SHATTERING IRA
MISCONCEPTIONS

JANAe,

MAy this Book help
You with YOUR IRA
TRAPS.

  YOUR GUIDE,
  Eric Scott

Shattering IRA Misconceptions

Eric L. Scott

Credits:
Writing –
Authored by Eric L. Scott
Writing Consultation by Paul Scott
Editing –
Edited by Lola Dunn
Cover Art –
Alexander Vultchev
Illustration –
Justine Huddleston

ISBN: 0692355960
ISBN-13: 9780692355961

Dedicated to my son Paul
Without his help and persistence,
it never would have happened.

What People are Saying About Eric's First Book:
The Five Crossroads: Unlocking the Secrets to Your Retirement Journey

"This is an excellent book for all pre-retirees considering retirement or those already in retirement. The use of well-known characters to shed light on legacy planning, taxation, low-risk investment management, income planning and long term care is carefully crafted by [Eric Scott]. Very well done. A must read."
– Drew Horter, Founder/Chief Investment Strategist at Horter Investment Management

Clients of Eric Scott Financial:
"When you believe that knowledge is power or money is power, do yourself a favor and spend the brief time it will take you to read [Eric Scott's] book…It will be time well spent."

"Eric Scott wrote the most helpful book on retirement I have ever read. The principles are sound and proven. The way it is presented in such a simple and relatable form enables anyone to be able to understand the precepts. It is a must for anyone wanting to have a comfortable and worry-free retirement."

"This is a great book to read to start your journey to financial freedom. Eric's book is so different from other financial books in that the five crossroads helps you understand the importance of building a strong financial foundation. Just like every great building, our financial houses need to be built correctly and this book will show you how it's done. Such a common sense way of looking at our financial success. If you read only one financial book, definitely read this one!"

TABLE OF CONTENTS

A NOTE FROM THE AUTHOR

WE LIVE IN AN AGE of information overload. That overload hurts us the most when dealing with our money and investments. One topic in particular, at least in my opinion, tends to be more misunderstood than most: IRAs and similar accounts.

Currently with over 17 trillion dollars in America that are invested in IRAs, 401(k)s and other similar accounts, I am often concerned with how misinformed people are about these accounts.

I wrote this book to answer the questions that I hear almost daily as a financial advisor. My goal is to teach people the important truths regarding their IRAs so they can make educated decisions when managing them.

Whether you're thinking about investing in an IRA, or you have a few already, I believe this book will help you with a better understanding of what having an IRA *really* means.

FOREWORD

SHATTERING IRA MISCONCEPTIONS IS FAR and away one of the finest financial books I have ever read. I have read hundreds of books and related articles in my 32 years in the investment and financial advisory business. It clearly reviews the 13 misconceptions and misunderstandings readers may have with respect to IRAs, 401(k) plans, 403 plans, SEP, TSPs (Thrift Savings Plans), etc.

The easy to read storybook format is perfect for both the expert investor and novice investor alike. The Guide serves to educate and clarify these misconceptions. Once you start to read it, you will not want to put it down. It may also help you to understand how competent, or perhaps incompetent your current advisor is.

The book begins with the Guide helping a couple understand the law changes affecwting IRAs and the history of IRAs and Roth IRAs.

Within the context of the history of the tax-deferred IRAs the Guide leads the couple through their IRAs actually have a "sharing agreement" with an "Unwanted Partner." These Unwanted Partners can change the taxation and distribution rules at any time. So who controls what, is the real question here.

How do you "buy out" and get rid of this Unwanted Partner? If someone is trying to take some of your income and IRA assets, this book helps you get rid of them.

This book helps you understand "bracket creeping" and how to avoid unnecessary taxation. Pretend this is a football game and you are on the 20-yard line of the opponent and you willingly take a 15-yard penalty knowing with 100% certainty you will score a touchdown in the next couple of plays. Playing the IRA game to your advantage is what is key here.

Remember, the IRA holders do not control the income, distribution and tax game now. So, the book teaches you how to strategize to win the game with your specific goals and needs. Here is where the book shows the reader unequivocally that "IRA knowledge is power."

Pre-retirees and retirees must read the middle chapters several times and rely on a competent, knowledgeable Fiduciary Advisor to give you the answers you need to fit your retirement plan.

One of the first chapters could be the most powerful chapter in the book to protect clients from assuming all is OK when they could be in serious financial danger.

There are great IRA analogies explained in the book. One is when the couple is taken on a mountain climbing expedition. It explains the climb up the mountain is equally important as the climb down. This is truly outstanding. Investing and accumulating IRAs etc. are important but how to distribute these Qualified Assets is equally important.

Don't make the mistake of having a huge percentage of your Required Minimum Distribution taken by the Unwanted Partner.

When moving IRA accounts from multiple accounts or custodians it becomes onerous, confusing and not simple and straightforward. How to manage these assets in a consolidated format is made clear to this couple. A cohesive well understood plan of managing and investing these IRA assets for the eventual distribution is critically important.

The book shows how income and tax planning are also very important. It is not what you make; it is what you keep. The author does a wonderful job of explaining this.

Keep your Unwanted Partner out of your pocketbook, clear and simple. Define your income sources on a taxable and non-taxable basis.

There is nothing better than to fire the Unwanted Partner and never have to deal with them again. Take control of your financial future with a qualified Fiduciary Investment Advisor Representative who has to put your best interests first.

The good thing is "you are living longer." The bad thing is "you are living longer." What do I mean by that? It's great to live to 90 or longer but what if you make unwise IRA financial decisions (or non-IRA assets)? It could leave you or your spouse financially destitute.

Most people do not equate legacy planning with their IRAs. The book explains that concept very well. How can you pass along your IRA to your children or grandchildren in the most efficient manner?

What do you have for beneficiaries; spouses, children, grandchildren? Are the IRA assets being passed to the beneficiary in a tax efficient manner? What is a multigenerational plan or a "Stretch" IRA? What about making appropriate beneficiary changes if someone dies? There are many unintended horror stories about IRA documents with no beneficiaries, ex-spouses (still as beneficiaries), and dysfunctional children receiving IRA inheritances. A competent Fiduciary Advisor can help clients make better, more informed decisions. The book makes this easy to understand.

At the end the author summarizes the financial future of the couple. The Financial House concept is truly the author's genius at work.

Looking for an advisor? What are the choices?

* An Insurance Agent (cannot do total investment management)
* A broker with a big Wall Street firm (with a lesser standard of care that is commission and transaction based)
* A bank employee registered representative
* An Independent Registered Representative with a regional or national planning firm (a lesser standard of care)
* An Independent Fiduciary who care about your best interest

Which one would you prefer?

This book if fabulous, easy to read, and focused. The couple is clearly directed through a myriad of IRA misconceptions to help them manage their IRA, 401(k), 403(b) or TSP or any qualified plan investing.

Your search for the answers are here. Eric Scott is the author and the expert. Eric's simplistic and straightforward approach gives the reader a complete set of guidelines to follow.

P.S. Don't forget to read the 2014 Tax Law Change Bonus Misconception

-Drew K. Horter, CFP™
Founder & President
Horter Investment Management, LLC
An SEC Registered Investment Advisor
Since 1991

THE LETTER

D EAR RYAN AND KATIE JOHNSON:
Your IRA account has sprung a leak. You could currently be losing thousands of dollars because the laws available to cork that drain are cleverly hidden. By not understanding your IRA completely, you could let your precious investments slip right through your fingers.

Did you know that as of 2012, an estimated 48.9 million U.S. households owned IRAs?[1] It may be one of the most common financial investments made in the United States, but it's also one of the most cleverly disguised and misunderstood. IRAs are so wrapped up in layers of jurisdiction, amendments, and fine print, that you're not likely to begin to untangle the mystery. At least not alone.

That's why I'm here to help. I'm offering you a unique opportunity to shatter 13 misconceptions about your IRA that are cleverly hidden in the fine print.

I challenge you to consider what you've read and attend an event uniquely catered to your needs at the following address:

123 Retirement Drive

---

1 Investment Company Insitute. http://ici.org/faqs/faq/faqs_iras/

As with any major financial decision, it's important to work with your spouse on your retirement plan. Please come together.

The cost to you: nothing. The benefits of visiting with me are unlimited if you are willing to learn. Don't lose any more vital time. Come and learn the hidden secrets to improving your financial situation throughout your retirement years.

The Guide

The Guide

⌣

Ryan and Katie Johnson sat nervously at the conference table at 123 Retirement Drive, scanning the room. The table stretched down the length of the room, adorned with a bit of foliage in the center. The walls held pictures of various presidents and founding fathers throughout history, and on one side stood a broad window covered by thick tan curtains, drawn closed, despite the welcoming day outside.

Ryan ran his hand through his brown hair streaked with grey. His sharp nose would have made his face severe were it not for his light almond eyes and jovial smile. Katie smoothed her dress over her knees and tucked her soft blonde hair behind her ears as she gave Ryan a gentle smile. One would hardly believe they were a couple in their 70s.

They were uneasy. They weren't entirely sure why the letter had drawn them to come here; they only had a distinct feeling that they sorely needed help.

They'd brought a small box which sat next to Katie's feet under the table containing several files: their IRA and 401(k) statements. They wondered how their mysterious host could help them and even less of what was in store.

The door behind them opened and they turned to see a man in a navy blue suit and tie. He was tallish, with slightly balding combed-back hair that was still deep brown despite his age. He smiled at both of them warmly.

"Welcome Mr. and Mrs. Johnson," the man said, shaking their hands in turn. "It's a pleasure to meet you. You may call me the Guide."

"The Guide?" Katie asked. "That's all?"

"Yes, the Guide will suffice. You see, I believe retirement is a journey with many paths to take. Rather than considering myself an advisor, doling out wisdom and sending you on your way, I consider myself a guide, a man who takes the journey beside you."

Katie blinked with surprise.

"What brings you to my office?" he inquired with a smile that intimated he already knew the answer.

Ryan pulled the letter they had received from their file box, smoothed it out, and set it on the conference table. "Well, as your…uh… warning so aptly pointed out," Ryan began, "we're in over our heads with our IRAs." Ryan sheepishly glanced at Katie. "We know enough to get by, I guess, but we figured we could both stand to learn a lot more so we don't make misinformed decisions in the future."

"Good. That's why I'm here. Before we get started, I have one question, the Guide began. "Do you both have IRAs?"

"I have a few," Katie replied, instinctively reaching for the file box to produce a few disheveled papers.

"I chose to invest in my company's 401(k) instead," Ryan added, trying to sound proud.

"Wonderful," the Guide said. "I want you to know that 401(k)s and IRAs are very similar investments. Other similar investments are 403(b)s, 457s, SEPs (or Simplified Employee Pensions), and

TSPs (or Thrift Savings Plans). There are others, but these are the most common."

"Okay," Ryan said, nodding.

"I mention this because I'm going to use the umbrella term 'IRA' throughout our conversation today, but unless I say otherwise, the same laws, rules and regulations will apply to all of the accounts I named," he explained in a matter-of-fact tone.

"That makes sense," Ryan said.

"So tell me," the Guide said, taking a seat opposite them at the table, "what makes you feel out of your element with regard to your IRAs?"

"Well," Katie ventured, "I suppose we just don't know much about them beyond the bare basics. I'm sure there are some laws or regulations about them that we may not have seen yet."

Well, certainly," the Guide said, leaning down to find something beneath the table. He slapped a thick stack of papers on the top of the desk with a sudden thud. "Take a look at this, for example. It's around 100 pages long and includes just some of the crucial details you need to know about your IRA to get by."

Ryan began thumbing through the small-printed pages with worry marking his forehead.

"In order to truly understand your IRAs and other qualified accounts, it's necessary to know the IRS Publications. I'm sure you've read the three that contain the majority of the information you need, the 560, 575 and 590?" the Guide asked archly.

Ryan and Katie exchanged quizzical glances and answered with blank stares at the stack of papers in front of them.

The Guide added with a smirk, "Did I mention that this is just the first section of three? This is only the IRS 590 law."

Ryan stared for a moment. "To be honest," he stammered, "I've never even heard of them before."

The Guide laughed, "I had a feeling you hadn't. *They* don't expect that you have seen them either. Within these three publications are pages upon pages of information specifically regarding IRAs and the qualified accounts that I mentioned before."

"I've never understood what the term 'qualified' means," Katie said.

"Ah yes. A qualified plan is a tax-deferred account for which you receive a tax deduction for investing. Your growth is tax-deferred. However you must begin withdrawing your money by the age of 70½, and that's when you'll begin paying taxes on not only the money you invested but also the growth you've experienced."

"Okay," Katie nodded, feeling a little more curious than when they entered the office.

"Let me back up a bit," the Guide said, "back to where it all began." To understand IRAs better, it's important to know the history surrounding them and the law changes that have occurred over the years. That's why I'd like to take you on a little journey."

Ryan and Katie looked puzzled.

"What do you mean by 'journey'?" Ryan asked, glancing at the four walls around them.

"We'll just take a simple walk through history to see where the IRA originated in the government and how it has developed since then. After all, if you want to beat opponents at their own game, you need to know everything, from the first play down to the very last," the Guide replied with a smirk.

"Okay," Ryan said, looking at his wife for reassurance. "I guess we can do that."

"Yes," Katie said, grasping her husband's hand. "I think I'm ready."

"Good," the Guide said. "Hold on tight."

With a swift motion, he grabbed the curtains covering the broad bay window and threw them open. A blinding light quickly made Ryan and Katie shield their eyes, still squinting to see as the Guide became little more than a shadow against the white brilliance. The room began to spin around them, and they lost themselves in the bright whirl.

A RETURN TO HISTORY

THE CONFERENCE TABLE WHERE THEY sat only moments ago had vanished and the Johnsons found themselves in the middle of the White House, and more specifically the Oval Office. Curiously, it too had a broad bay window adorned with thick tan curtains. Ryan opened and closed one side of the curtains to assure himself they were real.

"Are we… where I think we are?" Katie asked.

"Yes," the Guide replied. "You're standing in the White House. And the real question isn't where you are, but when."

"*When?*" Ryan repeated, confused.

"I'm glad you asked," the Guide said with a playful grin. "The date is September 2, 1974."[2]

Ryan and Katie looked around in disbelief. The Guide motioned to the desk in the room where they now saw a man with thinning hair sitting hunched over signing some papers. He glanced up with piercing blue eyes and a charming, thoughtful smile, yet he didn't seem to notice the three figures in the room, watching him with great curiosity.

---

2 United States Senate Special Committee on Aging. http://aging.senate.gov/crs/pension7.pdf

"It's Labor Day, to be precise," the Guide continued. "The man sitting before you is President Gerald Ford, and the document he's signing is the **Employee Retirement Income Security Act**, otherwise known as **ERISA**."

"You mean that's really President Ford?" Katie asked. "I can't believe we're standing here watching him approve a new law."

"Yes, that's really President Ford," the Guide said. "I told you we were returning to history, didn't I?"

"I thought you meant you were going to explain it," Katie said, still reeling from the bizarre turn of events.

"I chose to take a more literal approach," the Guide said, relishing her surprise.

"So here we are: Labor Day, 1974, a day not only about this President, but also about the law he's enacting. This day commemorates the birth of the IRA," he said with a flourish of enthusiasm. "Americans who were saving for retirement could now contribute up to $1,500 of their hard-earned money into an IRA each year. However, back then, when pensions were more common for the majority of American workers, only those without the coverage of a qualified pension could participate."

"Sounds like a good deal to me," Ryan said.

"And perhaps it was," the Guide said, "but the government added a personal advantage, and set it up as a win-win situation. They enticed American workers to save for their own retirement by allowing them to contribute money without paying the tax up front. However, in most cases, you couldn't withdraw that money from your IRA before 59½ without paying a substantial penalty. At age 70½, you were – and still are – required to start taking distributions known as RMDs (or required minimum distributions) using a formula created by the government. Instead of taxing the deposits going into your smaller accounts when you're starting out, the government could now tax fully grown, matured accounts that proved to be much more lucrative."

"Incredible," Ryan said, furrowing his brow. "So we benefit from the deferred taxes on our IRA investments, and the government benefits from taxing us in a potentially higher tax bracket later on."

"That's correct," the Guide said, "but that's not even the best part for the government. Imagine you're a farmer. The government tells you that you can either pay tax on the seed before you plant it, or you can pay tax on the crop when it's harvested." The Guide reached into his pocket and held out a wheat seed in his hand. "The seed represents the assets you invest in an IRA; the crop represents those assets plus the growth you see through the years." With that, the Guide pulled back the curtains to the Oval Office to reveal, not the grounds of the White House, but a golden wheat field stretching out to the horizon. Ryan and Katie gazed out, feeling the full weight of the deferred tax. "If you defer paying tax on the seed, you have to pay tax on the crop," the Guide said, staring out with them. He replaced the curtains and turned back to the center of the room.

"Sounds like the government gets the sweeter end of that deal," Katie added in a miffed tone.

The Guide winked at Katie and continued, "We'll talk about that later. Now remember: this law was passed back in 1974. If we follow the history forward, we can see what changes have been made that affect your IRA today," the Guide said.

Once again, the Guide pulled back the curtain of the window, allowing a dense fog to envelop the room. Katie and Ryan coughed and stumbled forward to find their way in the mist toward the sound of voices. Finally, they could see a man with a Dutch Boy haircut sitting on a stiff wooden chair in front of a small table covered in stacks of papers.

Not noticing his three onlookers, the man adjusted his jean jacket, unbuttoned the top button of his white dress shirt and tapped his cowboy boots anxiously as he looked out over the crowd surrounding him. The crowd gathered around attentively with microphones and cameras.

"I can't believe this," Katie said, placing her hands on her cheeks. "Why, that's Ronald Reagan."

"That's right," the Guide said. "The year is now 1981, and we're at the Rancho del Cielo in California, President Reagan's vacation home and the location where he signed the **Economic Recovery Tax Act.**

"This law superseded ERISA by allowing all Americans to contribute to an IRA. It also raised the contribution limit from $1,500 to $2,000 every year, and even allowed the participants to contribute $250 each year for their non-working spouses."

Ryan nodded, impressed.

They watched the president lean down and sign the document.

"The next step on our journey is also one in which President Reagan plays an important part," the Guide said.

The fog rolled in again as if on cue, and they stumbled onto the perfectly groomed grass of the South Lawn at the White House. Again they saw President Reagan sitting, surrounded by politicians and press. They watched with great anticipation as he signed yet another important document.

"The year is 1986," the Guide said as the Johnsons watched with great interest. "The president signed **The Tax Reform Act** here and added income limits to his previous law. In order for a person covered by an employer's plan, or a pension, to contribute money to his IRA, he would have to earn less than $25,000 if unmarried or less than $50,000 for a married couple filing jointly."

"Were there really that many changes in just a little over ten years?" Ryan asked.

"That's right," the Guide answered, "and there are even more by the time we catch up to 2014. Are you ready to move on?"

"Lead on," Ryan said, holding tightly to Katie's hand as they once again clambered through the fog. They found themselves in the Oval Office once again. This time the man at the desk was President Bill Clinton.

"It is 1996 and the document he's signing is the **Small Business Job Protection Act,**" the Guide said as Ryan and Katie watched President Clinton add his signature to the document. "A few parts of this Act affected IRAs and other similar accounts. First, the act created a new, more simplified 401(k) retirement plan which allowed small businesses to offer 'pension' plans to their employees with greater ease.

"Also, the limit for contributing to a non-working spouse's IRA was increased from $250 to $2,000 annually. Couples could now contribute together nearly twice what they could previously to their IRAs."

"I remember," Katie said. "That was very helpful when it came time to put money into my IRA."

"Likewise," the Guide added slyly, "the government stood to reap double the reward. They implemented even more helpful changes in the following years," the Guide said. Ryan and Katie closed their eyes, expecting the fog to roll in, but it never did.

Instead, President Clinton stood and moved very quickly out of the room. The room remained the same as various people rushed in and out, placed paperwork on the desk, or sat on the couches and discussed political matters. It was almost like pressing fast forward on an old VCR. Finally the speed slowed, and

President Clinton once again sat at his desk, leaning down and signing another document.

"We find ourselves in 1997, less than a year later," the Guide said. President Clinton is signing the **Taxpayer Relief Act**."

"I like the sound of that," Katie said brightly. "After all, we taxpayers could always use a little relief. How did the law change IRAs, though?"

"Well," the Guide said, "for starters, they raised the income limitations so more people could qualify to contribute to an IRA. Single taxpayers could now contribute if they made under $40,000 and a married couple could contribute if they made under $160,000 jointly."

"That's wonderful," Katie said.

"But that's not all," the Guide said. "With this law, we also saw the creation of a new type of IRA – the **Roth IRA**. This new type of IRA allowed you to pay tax on your money prior to investing and bypass taxes on the growth, withdrawals, and would pass tax-free to your heirs if you followed all the guidelines correctly."

"Now that sounds more like it," Ryan exclaimed.

"There's one more stop along the way before we can address the important information regarding your present day IRA."

With that, the people in the room again began to fast forward until President Clinton left the office and President George W. Bush entered. When the scene around them slowed, they watched President Bush make his way to his desk and sit down, smiling as he signed a document.

"The year is 2001," the Guide said as Ryan and Katie strained to see the document he was signing, "and the document you are witnessing President Bush sign is the **Economic Growth and Tax Relief Reconciliation Act.** Of course, you most likely know it as part of the Bush Tax Cuts.

"This law not only raised the contribution limits for IRAs but also, recognizing that older American workers have the ability to save more, allowed individuals closer to retirement a chance to play catch-up with their contributions as well. That meant American workers over 50 could contribute additional money above the limits placed upon everyone else."

"Those are some amazing changes," Ryan said, "and all in just a little over twenty five years."

"And those are just a few of the major changes. The laws change more and more as time goes on. For now, let's get back to the present and talk more about IRAs today." The Guide dramatically swept back the tan curtains, allowing the same brilliant light to surround them.

When the light began to dim, they found themselves back at the Guide's office, sitting in the conference room around the table where their journey began.

"Well, now that we have the historical background taken care of, I'd like to shatter some of the most commonly believed IRA misconceptions and share some of the disguised information everyone should know about IRAs," the Guide said, straightening his tie, "along with answering any questions that arise."

"Fine by me," Katie said. Ryan nodded in agreement.

"The IRA is one of the most popular retirement plans for investors," the Guide said. "However, it's also one of the most misunderstood investments. The most important thing for you to understand is that the IRA is a very ..." the Guide paused, carefully choosing his words, "unique investment."

"How so?" Ryan asked.

"Contributions to your IRA are tax-deductible and tax-deferred. This is especially important if you feel tax rates are going down in the future because you'll pay tax at the rates that are in place when you begin your withdrawals rather than the rates you had when you invested your contributions. Based on recent trends, however, it may not be wise to rely on a tax decrease in the near future.

"Oh, that's true," Katie replied. "I never thought about it like that before."

"Well, now that we know the history, let's get down to the secrets," the Guide said. "With so many people getting their information about IRAs from internet sources, we've discovered some of the knowledge they're acquiring is inconsistent and inaccurate. People have so many misconceptions about what an IRA is, what it does, and what it doesn't do that it's hard to find the whole truth. That's why I'd like to share 13 misconceptions about your IRA." He lowered his voice and leaned in toward Katie and Ryan. "The ones you'll likely find hidden beneath all of those laws," he said, pointing to the looming stack of books resting on the table.

YOUR IRA BELONGS TO YOU

"I've had many couples visit me over the years, and I've pinpointed quite a list of misconceptions to my clients about their IRAs, 13 to be exact. Why don't we start with the first misconception:" the Guide said, "Your IRA belongs to you. In fact, quite the opposite is true."

"Now, wait a minute," Katie said, feeling a little frustrated. "Of course it belongs to me. It's my money I've been investing all these years, isn't it?"

"Yes, you're right," the Guide said. "It's your hard-earned money that you've saved and invested, no doubt expecting nothing but the best results. That's what makes investing in an IRA so appealing. After all, this specific type of account does have many advantages.

"We just mentioned that IRA contributions are tax-deductible on earned income, and tax-deferred. You don't have to pay tax until you're required to make yearly withdrawals at age 70½."

"That's why I invested the way I did," Katie said.

"What many people fail to see, however," the Guide said, "is that investing in an IRA is much like starting a business with a partner, only with an IRA, your partner is the government. You see, with a regular business partnership, you would each contribute and have an equal say in running the business, but in this partnership, though you're the one putting the money in, the government holds majority control, or rather all the control because they could potentially change the laws at any time. The government is not merely your business partner when it comes to your IRA, they're your senior partner. From the moment you opened your IRA, you willingly signed over your rights and control to your personal retirement account."

"Our senior partner?" Ryan asked, suddenly concerned. "Are you sure about that?"

"It's funny you should ask," the Guide said. "Tell me, do you happen to know what IRA stands for?"

"Oh, of course," Katie said proudly, "Individual Retirement Account."

"Sorry to disappoint you. Though IRAs are commonly known as Individual Retirement Accounts, in Section 590 of the Internal Revenue Code, they are referred to as **Individual Retirement Arrangements.** The arrangement you agree upon puts you under some very merciless laws."

Katie and Ryan exchanged worried looks, considering the hidden terms of their own 'arrangements.'

"Allow me to share a story with you," the Guide said. "A lovely couple came in to see me a while ago. After retiring at 62, they had enjoyed several years of retirement when they met with me. The husband had a great pension, and they were receiving their Social Security checks. What's more, they were financially comfortable. They had just a little over half a million invested in an IRA, and they had taken out a Long-Term-Care Insurance policy just in case either of them needed special care later on. This couple truly believed they were set for life."

"I'm guessing the story doesn't end there," Ryan added. "What happened?"

"Well," the Guide continued, "I was able to visit with them and talk about their concerns regarding their financial situation, and the discussion eventually turned to the subject of their IRA."

The Guide pulled back the curtains of the window to reveal another version of the conference room. A man and woman stood, pacing the floor. The woman wrung her hands in anxiety, and her husband kept standing up and sitting back down every few moments. They seemed like an anxious couple waiting for an doctor's diagnosis rather than a couple at a financial meeting.

"You see how nervous they are?" the Guide asked. "That's because, for the first time, they're beginning to realize they don't have control of the money in their IRA. They can see that they are sharing ownership with the government, and by waiting to withdraw their RMDs at 70½, they may see the government take more of their IRA money than they had realized or planned on."

"I've always assumed you'd *want* to delay paying taxes on your IRA as long as you could. That's what I've been told for years," Katie said. "Is that a bad choice?"

"One very important thing you should remember is that there are no good or bad choices, and no right or wrong advice, per se, but rather the right advice for you as an individual. Each person's situation is different. Sometimes it's a great idea to postpone taxes on your IRA, other times it could be quite costly. There's no set right or wrong; it all depends on you and your particular situation. For instance, you may want to take your age and current tax bracket into account before making a decision. The most important component is having the knowledge you need in order to tell the difference. An informed decision will take you leaps and bounds beyond haphazard advice given without a strong knowledge base. You need someone who has traveled these mazes safely before. The right guide, if you will," the Guide said with a hint of pride in his voice as he straightened his tie.

Katie nodded, wondering privately if their situation could use a littler redirection.

The Guide continued. "In the case of the IRA, remember that the government is your senior partner. That means they make the rules. They control when you take your money out, how much you have to take out, and perhaps most dangerous of all, they have the voting rights to change all the rules, laws and guidelines whenever they see fit."

"What do you mean they can *change the rules and laws?*" Ryan asked, confused. "Weren't the rules set when we opened the IRA?"

"Need I remind you of our historical expedition?" the Guide asked. "We just saw some of the major historical law changes made to the IRA in just a little over 25 years. If there's one thing you can be certain of with IRAs, it's their inherent uncertainty. You are unwittingly at the mercy of Big Brother."

"Wow," Ryan said, settling down and running a hand through his hair. "I guess I never saw it that way before. We really do have a senior partner."

"Something few people realize is that with the right guidance, you can 'buy out' your senior partner and take back control of your IRA money," the Guide said. "Buying out the government isn't free, but it may be worth the price to regain control of your IRA going forward."

"Let's do it now, then," Katie said, excitedly. "Let's take back control of our retirement accounts."

"Now, hold on," the Guide said, smiling at her enthusiasm. "Not so fast. There are taxes and other factors to think about any time you withdraw from your IRA."

He gestured to the worried couple through the window who had given up pacing and sat at the conference table, thumbing through some papers. "Remember our friends had $500,000 invested in an IRA. Let's take a look at their particular scenario."

"Okay," Ryan said.

"Our friends were in the 25% tax bracket and, just for this example, we'll say their RMD, or Required Minimum Distribution was $20,000." The Guide pulled out 20 crisp dollar bills and laid them out on the table in two rows. "I'm a visual man myself, so let's compare that to 20 dollars. When they withdraw their money from the IRA, the IRS will take their share. In a 25% tax bracket, that leaves our friends with only $15,000 of the original $20,000." The Guide removed five of the bills to put the amount in perspective. "That, of course, isn't taking individual state income taxes into account, should they apply. Depending on where you live, you could end up with a lot less than that."

Ryan stared at the bills in the Guide's hand as if he wanted to snatch them back.

"Then, with that first example in mind, let's imagine they wanted to buy out their senior partner by withdrawing more than just the $20,000. There's the possibility that withdrawing too much could bump them into a higher tax bracket. Could you imagine if instead of keeping $15,000 for every $20,000 you withdraw, you only kept $13,000 in a 35% tax bracket, or $12,000 in a 40% tax bracket?" The Guide swiped away three more bills, leaving a lonely 12 behind. "That's nearly half of *your* money, gone."

"So are you saying," Katie asked cautiously, "that depending on our financial situation, it may be better for us to take the amount in smaller withdrawals?"

"It may be," the Guide said. "Remember: no one's financial situation is exactly the same and it's important that you discuss your options with the right retirement guide. This couple," the Guide said, motioning to the window, "made misinformed decisions, without knowing the true ins and outs of their IRAs. In this case, because they were waiting until their IRAs had grown, they were potentially facing more taxes on their accounts. They had no idea how to proceed on their own. Like them, you may find it more efficient to begin withdrawing smaller amounts over time so those withdrawals are taxed within lower tax brackets. We'll talk a little bit more about that later. The tricky part is defining those subtle lines.

"There isn't a one-size-fits-all solution but through proper planning you can find the solution that works within the system for your best interest. The truth is not always in plain sight, hence the reason so many misconceptions about IRAs exist."

"I can see we need to look at this closely," Ryan said. "We need to understand all the options available to us and decide how much of our IRA money throughout our lives we're... comfortable... handing over to the U.S. Treasury Department, or like you said, our senior partner."

"Oh yes," Katie added. "I don't want to wait around for the government to make all of the decisions. I want to have the control, and I want it back as fast as possible."

"Well, you've come to the right place," the Guide replied. "That's exactly what we'd like to teach you to do."

YOU CAN AVOID THE TAX

⌒

"THE NEXT MISCONCEPTION I WANT to talk to you about is the belief that you can avoid the tax," the Guide said. "Unfortunately, in most cases, you can't. The IRS knows what they're doing when it comes to getting the money owed them."

"So why bother talking about it at all?" Ryan asked, throwing his arms up. "If there's nothing we can do to avoid the tax, then I'd rather not worry about it."

"Just hear me out," the Guide said, continuing. "You may not quite be able to fully beat the tax, but there is a way that you can take back control and possibly save hundreds, thousands or even hundreds of thousands of dollars in taxes based on how you handle the money in your IRA."

"How?" Katie asked curiously.

"Well, let's return to the couple we've been speaking about," he replied. The Guide pulled the curtain back again to reveal a much happier version of the couple, gratefully shaking hands with none other but their current counselor. Ryan's mouth dropped open, and he kept glancing from one version of the Guide to the other. "These are the shadows of the past, Ebenezer," he responded playfully to Ryan's awkward gaze.

"This couple did the right thing. When they realized that they had a senior partner in the government, they wanted to get rid of that partner and take back control. So how do you get rid of a partner in business? You buy them out. As nervous and stressed as they were in our previous example, I had a chance to sit down with them, and we developed a strategy to withdraw their money a little bit earlier, and they were able to save taxes."

"How do you do that, though?" Katie asked.

"Taking their current income into account, we created a plan to take back control of their IRA. We soon discovered the most tax-efficient way to get rid of their senior partner was to withdraw the money and put it elsewhere.

"There are actually several different options when you're looking to buy your partner out. First, you can withdraw the money all at once, like ripping off a bandage. You'll feel the sting of higher taxes, but the senior partner will be gone in one fell swoop.

"Another option is to simply delay the process entirely. If you take out your RMDs on schedule in the minimal withdrawals from your IRA accounts, you're likely to pay more taxes and have that senior partner until you die."

Katie gulped nervously.

"A final option is buying the partner out over time. That's where I come in. This couple elected to do just that, in one of the most tax-efficient ways possible. Instead of withdrawing all the money at once, which would bump them into a much higher tax bracket, we found that it would be better tax-wise for them to withdraw the money in smaller increments over a few years to keep the tax in lower brackets."

"Isn't that what the RMDs do, anyway?"

"Well, yes and no," the Guide said. "You see, rather than just taking out their RMD amounts, we advised them to take out as much as they could without pushing their total income into the next tax bracket. That way they could potentially save money by paying tax in a lower tax bracket now. If you maximize your withdrawals for tax efficiency, you can withdraw your money quickly without paying any additional taxes. It may not seem like much, but let's not forget the difference even one tax bracket can make." He pulled his dollar bills from his pocket and tapped them on his palm. "Remember, if you pay tax on $20,000 in the 25% tax bracket, you'll keep $15,000. If you pay tax on that same amount in the 35% bracket, you'll only keep $13,000. If you're looking at five years of this trend, you will have paid an additional $10,000. In ten, you will have paid an extra $20,000. No one can afford to throw that kind of money away."

"Should we start withdrawing our money now?" Katie asked eagerly.

"Now, let's wait a minute," the Guide replied. "Everyone's financial situation is different. Say you visited a doctor for some flu-like symptoms. Would he use the same diagnosis and prescription for you as he did for a patient who came in with similar symptoms? Would he ignore the patient's past medical history or current medications? Of course not! He would make his diagnosis after carefully analyzing your personal situation. Financial guidance works the same way. The best solution for this couple isn't a universal remedy for what ails the financial world. If it was that simple to figure out, no one would be making misinformed decisions. This couple's situation is purely an example."

"We understand," Ryan said.

"As I was saying," the Guide began again, "the IRS knows what they're doing when it comes to taxation. Regardless of how hard you try to maneuver around them, the laws of the IRA are about as iron-clad as they come.

"Remember, if you look at the government as a senior business partner, it's for life, and the IRA contract expires upon the death of the investor. Unless you change it now, they will get the full value of what's owed them. If you don't pay it during your own life, the tax will be carried over to your beneficiaries when they inherit your IRA. I'm getting ahead of myself, though."

The Guide took a moment to gather his thoughts.

"With this couple," the Guide continued, "we determined that it was more tax-efficient to pay fewer taxes over a handful of years than to pay the tax in a higher bracket all at once. This saved them tens of thousands of dollars in taxes and gave them more money for retirement. This method worked for them, but the options and strategies need to be tailored specifically to you to really work to your advantage."

"I can see why we need to work with a guide," Katie said.

"That's right," Ryan added. "This will help us strike just the right balance To develop a program to maximize our withdrawals and minimize our taxes."

The Guide jumped in, "The end result will be more money in your pockets and a clear-cut route straight through the maze of IRA laws. You don't avoid the tax, but you can certainly pay much less with proper planning. Now, it's up to you. You decide how much you want to avoid in taxes and how soon you want to fire your senior partner."

You Can't Withdraw Money Early Without a Penalty

⟋⟍

K ATIE BIT HER LIP PENSIVELY as the Guide concluded. She looked up at Ryan and said, "Well, should we ask?"

"There's no harm at this point," Ryan replied, shrugging his shoulders.

"Our son has run into a little bit of financial trouble recently and he needs some money," Katie said apologetically. "We're not in a position to help him more than we already have. He has money invested in his own IRA, but he's only 50 years old, and he doesn't want to pay any penalties for early withdrawals."

"That sounds like a frustrating circumstance," the Guide said. "Life can often throw curve balls our way that can greatly affect our finances."

The Guide sat back a moment to think.

"As you mentioned, because he's only 50, he's subject to the 10% early withdrawal penalty, which applies to those who withdraw money before age 59½."

"Yes, this circumstance is quite difficult for him," Katie said, "especially knowing the money is available but he can't touch it without paying a penalty."

"What you and your son may not be aware of," the Guide said, smiling, "is that there are **several exceptions to the penalty.** I'd like to share them with you."

He made his way to the window once more and pulled back the curtains. They found themselves staring into a past version of the conference room once more. The Guide beckoned them closer.

They gathered around the window, watching a couple about their son's age, sitting at the table. Their conversation was thick with worry as they expressed their concerns to a younger version of the Guide sitting across from them.

"My, my," the present version of the Guide said, "I had so few grey hairs back then."

Ryan and Katie chuckled knowingly.

"My husband," the woman at the table said, "had a major surgery a few months ago, and we're not financially prepared to handle the bills that are rolling in."

"If only the bills could wait a few more years to be paid until I reached age 59 1/2," the man added, clearly worried, "we'd be able to pay our portion of the surgery with some of the money I have in my IRA."

Ryan and Katie exchanged silent glances, relieved that the couple's situation was not their own. "You see," the Guide said, "your son isn't the only one. Anyone could run into trouble before their IRA money is available. This couple came to me at 50 years old, worried that they would lose a lot of their retirement savings in order to avoid medical debt.

"Luckily, they had an escape clause. Little did they know that there is an exception to the Early Distribution Rule. As of 2014, you can withdraw money from your IRA early, if you use the money to pay for medical expenses that exceed 10% (or 7.5% if you're 65 or older through Dec. 31, 2016[1]) of your AGI, or Adjusted Gross Income.[2]

"Just to clarify," Ryan jumped in, "what does the Adjusted Gross Income actually entail?"

"Of course," the Guide replied. "Your adjusted gross income is defined as the total income i.e. wages, interest, dividends, pensions, etc. minus any deductions such as capital losses and IRA deduction and before any of your Schedule A itemized deductions or exemptions like IRA contributions, student loans, moving expenses, etc. Remember, laws can change even from year to year, so it's important to work closely with your retirement guide.

"Of course, there are other exceptions as well. There's one for your beneficiaries if you pass away, another for disability, and one for first-time homebuyers."[3]

"Hmm," Katie said. "That's good to know for future reference, but our son's problem doesn't fit any of those situations. He recently lost his job, and he's had trouble finding another one in this economy. If he had access to the money in his IRA, he'd be able to simply retire and live off the distributions. He'd rather not worry about rejoining the workforce, but the laws are making it difficult for him to start his retirement years early."

"Well, he'd love to hear about this! There's a segment in the IRC, or Internal Revenue Code, that's not very well known," the Guide said. "It's in Section 72, Part T,[4] which we simply call 72t. Remember the IRC, also known as the Tax Code, has around 4

---

1 IRS. http://www.irs.gov/Individuals/2013-Changes-to-Itemized-Deduction-for-Medical-Expenses

2 IRS. http://www.irs.gov/taxtopics/tc502.html

3 IRS. http://www.irs.gov/taxtopics/tc557.html

4 Section72.com http://www.section72.com/html/72_t_.html

million words[5] and can be overwhelming for the American tax-payer to read, let alone understand. For example, have you ever read *War and Peace?*"

"I have," Katie said hesitantly, "but it took me a while. That book is over 1,000 pages long and a bit dry. It doesn't help that every other character's name is Smernikov," she said with a laugh.

"Well," the Guide said, "this might be a fun fact for you. The U.S. Tax Code has as many words as seven copies of *War and Peace.* And trust me, it's much drier."

"Wow," Katie said. "That *is* overwhelming. Okay, rather than read it, I'll just ask. What is the 72t and how can it help our son?"

"Oh yes. Section 72t discusses the optional plan for SOSEPP, or a Series of Substantially Equal Periodic Payments," the Guide said.

"That's a mouthful," Ryan said. "What does it mean?"

"In layman's terms," the Guide replied, "it means if you wish to have access to your IRA funds before reaching 59½, you can determine your yearly distribution from the IRA using a very specific table and then begin taking distributions. You have a chance to take out equal and periodic payments over that time. It's like a miniature version of your RMD when you hit 70½."

"So there's no catch?" Katie asked.

"The catch is that the distributions must be taken out for at least five years, or until your son reaches the age of 59½, whichever is later. At that time, he'll be eligible to take out distributions in any amount without penalty anyway. If he's concerned about spending his IRA money too quickly, he can reduce the amount taken when he starts receiving his Social Security check."

"How does he set up a plan like that?" Ryan asked eagerly.

---

5 Forbes. http://forbes.com/sites/kellyphillipserb/2013/01/10/
tax-code-hits-nearly-4-million-words-taxpayer-advocate-calls-it-too-complicated/

The Guide replied, "It's a rather delicate process. There are various methods to withdrawing equal and periodic payments through the 72t exception. It is important for anyone wanting to use one of these options to know which one best fits their situation. A retirement guide will help you find out which is best for you. Otherwise, you risk paying that 10% penalty. Believe me, this isn't a process you can just improvise and hope to stay afloat. It takes careful planning with a guide who knows these waters."

"We're starting to see that," Ryan said, smiling. "Thanks for the information. I can't wait to tell our son he can take income from his IRA without a penalty. We never would have known about all the options available!"

MISCONCEPTION #4

IT'S OKAY TO KEEP MONEY
IN YOUR 401(K)

"LET'S MOVE ON TO OUR next misconception," the Guide said. "It's okay to keep money in your 401(k)."

"Wait a minute," Ryan said. "Are you saying I shouldn't have money in my 401(k)? The company I worked for took very good care of me and part of the benefits package I was offered when I began working was the chance to contribute to a 401(k). My employer even matched my contributions up to a certain percentage, doubling what I put in. Why shouldn't I keep my money with them?"

"Now, I don't doubt for a moment that you had an excellent employer who did their very best to take good care of you," the Guide answered. "However, I do feel that you might be limiting your options. The average 401(k) that I see with my clients has only 15 to 25 investment options available."

"I felt like the options they offered were good investments, though," Ryan stated.

"And they very well might have been," the Guide said, "but what happens when they're not anymore? What happens when you stop benefitting from those investments or when an outside investment opportunity arises? You're still limited to the investments within your employer's 401(k) plan."

"Gee, I'd never considered that. I guess our investment needs have changed over the years. What options do I have to change it?" Ryan queried.

"You actually have a few. One option is rolling the account over into an IRA," the Guide replied. "Remember, a 401(k) limits the choices you can make regarding *your* investments. Say you walk into an ice cream shop that sells as many flavors as you can imagine. You have your heart set on Rocky Road, but the owner says you can only choose from vanilla, chocolate, strawberry, or sherbet. There's nothing wrong with the offered flavors, but with all the options out there, why settle? The same concept works for your 401(k) investment. Rather than sticking to the 15-25 investment options the company offers with a 401(k), it may better to work within a financial vehicle, such as the IRA or other similar accounts, which allow you to choose between hundreds of investment options. After all, it's your money. Shouldn't you have the ability to invest it the way you want to?"

"That makes sense, Ryan," Katie said, nudging him. "So was it a mistake for my husband to invest with them at all?"

"Not necessarily," the Guide said. "Remember, everyone's situation is different. For many people, investing in a 401(k) can be a wise decision."

"How so?" Katie asked.

"As with an IRA, the contributions are tax-deductible and tax-deferred. Also, just as you mentioned, many employers are willing to match your contributions up to a certain point. That means you may be able to double the investment amount going into your 401(k) account. We call this free money. Also, employers will often deduct the contribution directly from your paycheck before your pay day. It's a lot easier to save and invest money when it's saved and invested for you before you can even consider spending it. You don't need to do the leg work, and you never even have a chance to miss it."

"That sounds reasonable," Ryan said. "I'm glad I chose to invest in my 401(k) then."

"The important thing to remember is, at that time, investing in a 401(k) may have been a good decision, but might be limiting your current investment options," the Guide said. "The decision you need to make is whether you should keep your 401(k) after you retire or open up an IRA that offers you many more investment options."

Ryan nodded thoughtfully.

"Believe me, you're not alone in your curiosity about 401(k)s and the options they offer. In fact, many Americans have a large portion of their retirement savings in 401(k)s for the beneficial reasons we just discussed. Once you retire, though, the list of benefits we discussed start to dwindle. For one, your employer no longer matches your contributions."

"That's true," Ryan said. "I guess I hadn't considered that my 401(k) would ever change."

"And another thing," the Guide said, "your 401(k) may also limit your options for distributing your investments to your heirs in most cases. For example, your 401(k) may only offer a one-time payout or it may spread the payouts over the course of a year or even over five years as some of your main options. With other qualified accounts, you have many more options available to you. You could potentially choose to spread the payouts over your heirs' lifetimes, or you could possibly choose payouts that pass down your legacy through more than one generation through multi-generational options."

"Well," Ryan said tentatively, "those options do sound much better, but I'd rather not pay the taxes to take my money out of my 401(k) just to put it into an IRA."

"Well, Ryan, that reminds me that I haven't mentioned the best part!" the Guide exclaimed with gusto. "Very few people realize a very important fact. It's another of those hidden gems buried in layers of law. You actually wouldn't pay any tax to move your 401(k) to an IRA account. Because IRAs and 401(k)s are the same type of account and subjected to the same laws, you are able to transfer or rollover your money from a 401(k) to an IRA without any taxation."

"That certainly sweetens the deal!" Katie said with a gasp.

"And this doesn't only apply to those who are retired like yourselves," the Guide said. "Far too often, it's believed that once you've invested in a 401(k), you can't touch that money until you've retired and have reached the age of 59½. However, some companies have 401(k) plans that offer what is called an **in-service rollover** which allows you to move part of your current 401(k) investment into an IRA. You can do this regardless of your age, even while you're still employed with the company that offers you the 401(k). However, remember that every situation and every company is a little different. Many companies do have a specified age set in their 401(k) plan documents, and often that specified age is 59½.

"The important thing to remember is that there are specific procedures for an in-service rollover, and you must do it correctly to avoid the financial penalties and income taxes."

"This information is so helpful," Ryan said.

The Guide replied, "What it really comes down to is this: you want the freedom to invest your money where you want, the chance to potentially have more beneficiary options, and a way to open up some tax-free accounts. A 401(k) generally doesn't give you the same financial freedom because you're locked into fewer options in many areas, whereas investing in IRAs opens a window of possibilities to you."

"Wow," Ryan said. "I never would have thought that I may not want to keep my money in my 401(k). My investment options really have been limited. I can see we need to sit down and examine the options between my 401(k) and IRA accounts to make an informed decision."

The Guide replied, "It would certainly be wise to understand all your options in retirement."

YOU CAN ALWAYS TREAT YOUR IRA THE SAME

⌐⁓

"ONE OF THE MOST IMPORTANT things you need to realize is this: IRAs are very unique," the Guide said. "An IRA is a hybrid of two accounts: **growth and income**."

"I'd never thought of it that way before," Ryan said. "We've always just focused on trying to get our accounts to grow. Is there more to it than that?"

"Well, that's exactly my point," the Guide replied. "Growth is important, but that may no longer be your primary goal. After you retire, your IRA behaves differently than while you were working, so you just can't treat it the same way. Once you reach 70½, your IRA becomes a mandatory source of income."

"Why?" Katie asked.

"Well," the Guide replied, "many investors, while their investments are still in the **growth phase**, use a strategy known as 'buy-and-hold.' I'm sure you've heard phrases like 'the market will come back' or 'it's only a paper loss.'"

"Of course," Katie said. "We've used some of those phrases for comfort ourselves in tough investment times."

"When you truly understand IRAs," the Guide continued, "you'll see that once you reach age 70½, and your RMDs come rolling in, you're now in the **income phase**. At this point, should you suffer a loss, it's no longer a paper loss because you're required to withdraw funds from your IRA. There's no more time to wait for the market to come back. You're looking at a real loss.

"Consider this scenario," the Guide added, making his way to the window and sweeping the curtain back. Outside stood a tiny tree, a young sapling swaying in the wind. "Your IRA's lifetime is much like the growth of an apple tree with you as the keeper of the orchard. Your tiny seed of an account grows and grows through your working years. You struggle to save and grow your money for years, just as you would care for the life of a fruit tree."

Before their eyes, the apple tree began to grow. The tree sprouted more branches shooting off the main thickening trunk. Soon there stood before them a lovely apple tree with lush leaves, thick healthy bark and delicious, juicy apples hanging from the branches. Ryan and Katie smiled, considering the work they'd put into their own IRA savings.

"But, that's not all there is to do," the Guide noted. "When your harvest time arrives, it's time to reap your rewards and really focus on the income you receive through your RMDs. Let's face it, even though some people don't even want their RMDs, some count on it as income, and some decide to just throw it back into a bank account, those RMDs are ready for harvest whether you like it or not. At 70½, your RMDs are ripe for the picking."

As they continued to watch, a man in a straw hat and overalls ambled up to the tree outside. He took a look at the fruit, but instead of apple-picking, he began watering the tree and pruning some stray branches. He left when his work was done, and the apples began to fall. Soon the ground was littered with the wasted fruit, rotting needlessly in the dirt.

"You see, this farmer was so determined to continue growing his tree that he neglected to take care of the fruit when the harvest came around. Harvesting is how you prepare for your income. You need to prepare for that fruit before it hits the ground. Will you plan to spend the RMDs, reinvest them, place them in taxable, tax-deferred or tax-free accounts? At 70½, your major growth period is winding down, thus, you need to think about your accounts differently. Certainly, growth will always be a goal, but it shouldn't be your highest priority any longer. It's beneficial in this stage to be more conservative and focus on the income from your IRA, or the 'fruit' of your tree."

"Oh dear," Ryan said, "I never considered that waiting out a market turn-down could be so much riskier during retirement. It's true that we have no choice once the RMDs are in place. The money must be withdrawn, so I can see why we can't afford market losses."

"And, of course, the problem with believing the market will come back is that just because the market as a whole comes back, that doesn't mean every bond, mutual fund, and stock does. For example, WorldCom filed for bankruptcy in 2002, becoming the largest bankruptcy filing in American history up to that point. Another famous bankruptcy was Circuit City in 2008. These stocks didn't come back."

The Guide pulled out a stop watch, set it for one minute and turned it for Ryan and Katie to observe. The seconds began ticking down.

"You see, the 'buy-and-hold' strategy may work sometimes for other investments, but it's not the best strategy with regards to your

IRA because of the forced distributions. Holding out for the market with an IRA is like holding onto a ticking time bomb set to go off when you reach 70½ no matter what. Five, four, three, two, one."

As the time expired, the stop watch began a quick, relentless buzz.

"I never thought of it like that," Ryan said uneasily.

"You see, IRAs are designed to supplement your income in many cases. Why would you want to have a supplemental income that can potentially decrease in value when you're required to withdraw your money?"

"Why is it set up that way, then?" Katie asked.

"The federal government set the system up that way," the Guide said. "They're willing to give you some up-front benefits and wait patiently for you to reach the designated age because they're going to receive taxes on your entire crop, or growth, when you begin withdrawing your money. However, if the market value of your IRA goes down, they could potentially receive less tax revenue as well. Do you remember when the S&P 500 dropped approximately 37% in 2008? They passed a 1-year-only law stating that Americans weren't required to withdraw their RMD in 2009 because they wanted to give people the chance to grow their money back. Out of pure generosity no doubt…. Well, let's just say they too understand that this is a **growth and income** account. It allowed them to regrow their tax base."

"So do we have to rethink our entire financial plan?" Ryan asked with worry in his voice.

"Well, in regards to your IRA, you may," the Guide replied matter-of-factly. "Allow me to show you what I mean."

The Guide stood and walked over to the curtain. "You might want to put on your coats," he added over his shoulder as he pulled his lapels closer around his neck. He swept the curtain back quickly. Katie and Ryan didn't have time to feel puzzled. A strong blast of icy wind whipped through the conference room, as snow began to fall in from the wintery scene outside the window. A gigantic mountain towered outside. From their vantage point, they could see the mountain stretching far above and below them. They could see a few intrepid hikers clinging to the vast sides with ice picks, daringly scaling the mountain.

"What is this place?" Ryan asked, hugging Katie's shoulders as they approached the window.

"This," the Guide said, raising his voice over the rush of the wind, "is Mount Everest. Were you aware that about 240 deaths have occurred on Everest expeditions?"[6]

"I certainly believe it," Katie said, staring down at the steep sides.

"You'd be surprised to know that the climb up isn't where the majority of the deaths occurred. Most of them happened on the journey down."[7]

"I ne-ne-never would have guessed," Ryan said, his teeth chattering a bit. "B-B-ut what does it have to do with our IRAs?"

The Guide replaced the curtain with some effort and the howling wind and snow ceased. He brushed off his suit coat and ushered Ryan and Katie to the fireplace at the other side of the room.

"That mountain has more in common with your IRA than you think, Ryan. A death that occurs on Mount Everest is much like a financial 'death,'" the Guide said. "The journey up represents your career, your investing years, your savings, and all of your hard work. The journey down, on the other hand, represents your

---

6 History.com http://www.history.com/news/7-things-you-should-know-about-mount-everest

7 Science Daily http://www.sciencedaily.com/releases/2008/12/081209221709.htm

retirement years and the distributions required by the government. My point is you can't handle your investments the same in retirement as you did during your career. After you make it to the top, you still have to be careful on the way back down. You've worked too hard climbing to the summit with your saving and investing to risk potential losses from your retirement accounts on the way down. The journey down requires a different kind of thought and effort."

The Johnsons nodded.

"A lot of people, just like these hikers, lose money due to the manner in which they invested in their IRAs, and yes, some even run out of money because the elements get the better of them. They not only battle against the forced withdrawals, taxes, inflation, and their own investment decisions, but also many people have cause to worry about their longevity and the fact that they could outlive their money. With all of these factors working against them, they wind up financially dead at the bottom of their personal Everest, defeated because they never learned the laws and never sought out a guide who would show them the safe way to climb back down.

"Wow, I can really see the danger of attempting this alone," Katie said, feeling the weight of the example.

"Your IRA can no longer be treated like a growth account. In retirement, it transitions to an income account, an account you need to primarily preserve. It's important that you treat it as such by investing differently, specifically in conservative, low-risk, safe and secure accounts. I use a philosophy I like to call the **financial house**."

"Financial house?" Ryan repeated, curious.

"The financial house is a term I use to explain how to invest your accounts and protect your assets. Like building a regular house, there are many steps to building a financial house. You begin with what I call the cornerstones of protection for your personal assets and income, add a foundation of safe/secure investments, build walls with low-risk/low-volatility investments, and finally, when your situation is ideal, you top it all off with a roof of moderate-to-high-risk accounts. We'll talk about the financial house in more depth a little later."

Katie and Ryan exchanged thoughtful looks. Katie said, "I always just thought of my IRAs as growth accounts, but I can see now that they will be different when I turn 70½ and I'm required to use them for income. I know we need to look at our accounts differently and reevaluate how to use our IRAs. I just hope we haven't lost too many opportunities already."

"Let me assure you: many opportunities still lie ahead," the Guide replied warmly.

OVERLOOKING YOUR RMDS ISN'T A BIG DEAL

⌒⁀

"So, NOW THAT YOU KNOW your IRA deserves different treatment after retirement when it transitions from a growth account to an income account, let's discuss one of the most tragic pitfalls that can ensnare you."

Curious, Ryan and Katie leaned forward.

"A man came in to see me a while ago with some very unfortunate news," the Guide said. "He was 75 years old, so his IRA was already in its income phase. He had previously prepared all the paperwork for his Required Minimum Distribution, or RMD. He didn't want to send the papers in until the end of the year, though, so he saved the paperwork on his desk at home.

"The time drew nearer and, before this man had a chance to send the paperwork in, he suffered a heart attack. Fortunately, the attack wasn't too serious, but he spent three to four weeks in the hospital. By the time he returned home, the deadline to file his RMD paperwork, December 31st of that year, had passed and he was now subject to the Excise Tax."[8]

---

8 http://www.irs.gov/Businesses/Small-Businesses-%26-Self-Employed/Excise-Tax

"What's the Excise Tax?" Ryan asked nervously. "Is that the fine imposed on you when you're late withdrawing your RMD?"

"Yes, the fine is referred to as the Excise Tax. Here's what many people don't understand about it," the Guide replied. "They believe that it's a small fine that serves as a 'slap on the wrist' and a reminder not to forget next year. Many assume it's similar to a late fee for a mortgage payment, just a slight annoyance or a minor formality.

"What they don't realize is that the Excise Tax isn't small at all," the Guide said. "In fact, it's a fee equal to 50% of your RMD. That means, right up front, you lose half of the required withdrawal. On top of that, you're still required to pay income tax on the full amount. You'll be paying taxes on money that has already been taken away from you. In a 25% tax bracket, you'd be handing 75% of your RMD to the federal government out of the amount they forced you to withdraw in the first place. That amount could increase if you're required to pay state tax as well. In fact, under those circumstances, depending on your state and your federal tax brackets, you could potentially see more than 90% of your withdrawal taken away as tax."

"90%?" Katie asked. "Is that even legal?"

"That's just it, Katie," the Guide replied. "Not only is it legal, but it's what you willingly agreed to! It's all spelled out for you in the fine print of the tax codes. The hardest part for many people to swallow is that as owners of their IRAs, they agreed to the deadlines and rules associated with the account when they invested their money in the IRA, yet many at the time did not understand the severity of what could take place years later.

"We discussed the partnership between you and the government earlier, remember? When you first opened your IRA, you willingly agreed to the guidelines that have been set for you. That means the government is in control of when and how much money you must withdraw each year. If you miss the deadline, it's unfortunate but it's you who broke the terms of the 'contract.' As your senior partner, it's no skin off their nose if you didn't bother to read the fine print.

"In a way, you can compare it to purchasing a used car. That salesman does everything he can to shine up that car to look just like new. He's explaining everything to you right up until you purchase it. You may have been so wrapped up in the excitement of the buying experience that you missed reviewing the return policy. When the engine starts clunking a few days later, your salesman's hands are tied by the contract you signed just days before. It's the fine print that can cost you more than a pretty penny."

"Wow," Ryan said, rubbing his forehead as he tried to take it all in. "I guess we never saw it that way before."

"Well, the best lesson you can take away is that those RMD deadlines are more than crucial, and you need to safeguard against missing that RMD withdrawal. The first thing you can do is be prompt. Procrastination can be the downfall of any aspect of your retirement, but as you can see from our example, it can cost you more than you bargained for. It certainly did for the man who suffered the sudden heart attack.

"The safeguard, something this man could have done differently, is talking to the right retirement guide sooner. You see, when he came to me, it was too late. The Excise Tax had already taken its toll. Remember you have the option to use your investment company to your advantage. When you turn 70½ and your RMDs are required, your investment company can send you the paperwork so you can set up your distributions. Once the required distribution paperwork is in place, and you designate when to receive your RMD, it can then be set up automatically as a worry-free process.

On top of that, they can also calculate the distributions for you to make sure the numbers are correct, so you never have to worry. I believe this option is far better than the alternative – doing it yourself. Working with a retirement guide and your investment company ensures better accuracy and gives you peace of mind. Without them, you risk potentially losing thousands of dollars due to misinformed decisions. Those who choose to do it themselves run that risk. Is it worth it?"

"Certainly not," Katie said.

"Keep in mind that not every company or brokerage firm will set this up systematically or calculate it for you, so it's ultimately up to you to make sure you know what options your IRA company or brokerage firm provides."

"What if, even after all that, we still end up missing the RMD for a good reason?" Ryan asked.

"There's a waiver you can request when you file your taxes if you feel you had reasonable cause for missing the RMD. I recommend you use IRS Form 5329 and follow the directions for requesting the waiver."

"So there *are* valid reasons?" Ryan asked. "What are they?"

"Well, I've already shared one with you," the Guide said. "The man we just discussed suffered a heart attack. A serious medical condition could prevent you from being able to withdraw your RMD and is possibly a reason that could be considered.

"Another potential example could be that you inherited the IRA from someone who recently passed away and weren't sure when the RMD was due. There are several others as well, but remember the IRS isn't required to honor the tax waiver. It's up to them to determine which reasons are justified and which aren't. A word to the wise, you generally have just 12 months to get the paperwork turned in. I'll tell you right now, if you've missed an

RMD withdrawal in the past, they'll be far less likely to grant your request at another time."

"It sounds like the responsibility falls solely on us," Katie said.

"That's true," the Guide said. "Always remember that there's only one person who is responsible to make sure you take your RMD on time – and that's you."

"I see that we need to be particularly cautious about those RMD deadlines," Ryan added, considering his own upcoming deadline. "I won't take them lightly anymore."

"Good," the Guide said with a smile. "You're on the right track to making the best decisions for you and your IRA."

IT'S UNNECESSARY TO
CONSOLIDATE ACCOUNTS

"**O**H, I HAVE A THOUGHT," Katie said as she lifted their box onto the table and rummaged through the files. She shuffled the papers around for a few minutes and finally resigned herself to the fact that the papers she was looking for probably weren't there.

"Darn," she said, turning back to the Guide. "I think I must have forgotten the papers I wanted from one of my IRAs."

"You have quite a bit of paperwork in there," the Guide said, glancing over Katie's shoulder curiously, "if you don't mind my saying so."

"Well," said Katie, a little flustered, "we have quite a few accounts and sometimes it's hard to keep track of them all."

"I'll be candid with you," the Guide said. "That's a little worrisome. We've just discussed the huge impact forgetting your RMD can have on your accounts. With each additional IRA account you have, you increase the risk of missing an RMD withdrawal, and you could potentially cost yourselves hundreds or even thousands of dollars from the Excise Tax, not to mention the federal and state taxes."

"I guess you're right," Ryan said, "and the older we get, the less frequently we remember things."

"It's that way for all of us," the Guide replied with a chuckle.

"You know," Katie said, "now that you mention it, I'm not sure why I have so many IRAs."

"Well," the Guide said, "take comfort in knowing you're not alone. In fact that's more normal than you'd think. Many of the people I visit with, whether single or married, are attempting to juggle an average of six IRAs."

"How does that happen?" Katie asked.

"There are a number of reasons, actually," the Guide said. "Again, nobody's situation is exactly the same, so it'd be presumptuous of me to think I know everyone's reasons. However, I believe it's often because of the way opportunities present themselves throughout our lives."

"What do you mean?" Ryan asked.

"If I may, I'll give you an illustration." The Guide pulled back the plush tan curtains to reveal a quaint ice cream parlor, with a young man browsing the selection. "You see, you're investment opportunities are going to look much like this, with each option offering new, tasty aspects. Let's say you open your first IRA in your 20s because your advisor or CPA told you it was a good investment," the Guide said. "After all, when you're just starting out, the tax-deferred aspect of the account appeals to you."

"Right," Ryan replied.

With that, the young man purchased a single-scoop ice cream cone, confidently admiring his choice.

"Next, let's say you get into your chosen career and your company offers a 401(k). It's hard to say no to an employer matching your investment, isn't it?"

"That's why I opened mine," Ryan replied.

The young man purchased another ice cream cone with a different flavor. He started licking both cones intermittently.

"As the years go on, several other IRA opportunities arise, offering so much variety that you simply can't resist. You may have looked for an account yielding a higher interest rate and added additional IRAs. Maybe you wanted a spousal IRA. Perhaps you changed jobs and started another 401(k) and converted your previous 401(k) to an IRA."

The ding of the cashier's bell rang out repeatedly. The young man's purchases were adding up. He now held two cones in each hand with three more clutched in the crook of his elbow. He was frantically licking all of them, trying to keep them from spilling to the floor, while they slowly started to melt all over his hands.

The Guide closed the curtain on the unfortunate man with too much of a good thing. "In the end, all of those different flavors didn't benefit him. In fact, they were too much for him to juggle all at once. He would have been fine with his top three or four flavors. Instead he couldn't keep track of all of them and so he lost control. My point is that for whatever reason, many people start IRAs one after the other, and before they know it, they are 70½, retired, and potentially managing five to ten IRAs in their portfolios. And with that many melting ice creams in your hands, there's a higher chance that you'll miss a few drips along the way."

"Wow," Katie said. "That just seems overwhelming."

"It can be," the Guide said. "As you said yourself, Ryan, the older we get, the harder it is to remember things. It's not just about memory, though. It's more about peace of mind: the security that you won't wake up in a cold sweat one night wondering if that last, obscure RMD was taken out in time."

"Peace of mind, huh?" Ryan asked, curious.

"Yes," the Guide said. "During your career, you have to think about money constantly. In retirement, however, money is something you shouldn't have to worry about as much. Money should be simple so you can use it to enjoy your retirement, not an additional source of stress. The fewer accounts you have to manage, the less stress you'll have during your retirement years."

"Makes sense to me," Ryan said, nodding.

"I'll give you another example," the Guide said. "Another lady and her husband, much like the two of you, came in to visit with me. Over the years, they had acquired ten IRAs. Now, keep in mind, that doesn't include their other investments. On top of the ten IRAs, they had a few checking accounts, a savings account, some CDs, and a few other investments. Needless to say, they were overwhelmed trying to keep track of everything.

"The woman was quite upset when they met with me. She had opened up a CD with her bank, but, amidst the shuffle of her many accounts, she had forgotten that this particular CD was actually an IRA CD. You see, she was trying to juggle so many accounts, that she just couldn't keep up with the rules, regulations, and laws associated with each of them. Because of that oversight, she suffered a heavy penalty due to missing her RMD, an RMD she never realized existed. This mistake could have been easily avoided if they had come to me earlier. I could have reviewed and explained the conditions of each account. This simple step could have potentially saved them thousands of dollars by giving them the knowledge they needed to succeed."

"It's easy enough to recognize that we have too many accounts," Katie said, a little worried. "It's quite another to know what we should do about it. After all, we've already opened them. The damage is already done, right?"

"Well yes," the Guide said, nodding, "you're right. You can't change the past. What you can do, with the right guidance, is set things on the right track again."

"How?" Ryan asked.

"When this couple came in to visit with me," the Guide said, "they had ten IRAs as I said. After I'd talked with them for some time and learned about their financial situation and their needs, we were able to consolidate those accounts down to just three IRAs that they felt were necessary for their lifestyle and financial needs."

"I'm glad that worked for them, but I'm afraid that our situation might be a different story. Won't that cost us thousands of dollars in taxes when we pull the money out? I'm not sure we're willing to do that, especially if we're just consolidating them into more taxable accounts."

"Well, I'm glad you brought that up. Consolidating those accounts would cost them nothing! As long as it is done correctly, shifting money from one IRA to another is a transfer that is a non-taxable event. When you exchange money within the same types of accounts under the same laws, the transfers won't cost you anything in taxes. It's entirely a win-win situation that will likely bring you many benefits."

"Wow! That sounds like a wonderful idea. I guess it's time for us to evaluate how much we should consolidate," Katie said, confidently. "We could certainly use the peace of mind during our retirement years."

"I couldn't agree more," the Guide replied, reassuringly.

TAX SAVINGS STRATEGIES
WON'T WORK FOR YOU

"THIS BRINGS ME TO MY next point. Many people just blindly follow the protocols of their IRAs, never realizing the number of tax savings strategies available to them. You can't go into a game of chess without a strategy, so I'm here to share some strategies with you that will help you play the game."

"It sounds like a difficult game to play, especially when the government seems to have the upper hand. What can we do about it?" Katie asked with an edge of determination in her voice.

"Well, like we've said before, you can't avoid the tax in most cases, and you definitely can't avoid the RMDs. But, there are certain tax-saving strategies you can tap into to help you save taxes on the money you withdraw."

"So there's really no way around the tax?" Ryan asked.

"In most cases, no," the Guide replied. "When you start withdrawing money from your IRA, you will pay taxes on it. However, you can use a strategy that fits your unique situation in order to pay taxes more efficiently and, therefore, keep more money for yourself."

"How can we do that?" Katie asked.

"The important thing to remember," the Guide replied, "is that the total of your income, up to your last dollar determines your highest tax bracket. I'm going to base my example on the 2014 income tax laws for married couples filing jointly. However, the same strategy can apply to single filers or married couples filing separately. The numbers will just be different."

"Great," Ryan said.

"Let's see," the Guide paused in thought. He moved toward the wall and slid a panel over to reveal a white board. The Guide quickly drew a spigot on the board, followed by seven pails, each larger than the previous. He labeled each of them respectively, 10%, 15%, 25%, 28%, 33%, 35% & 39.6%. "Imagine that each tax bracket is like a water pail, with your money working as the water." He drew water pouring into the pails as he spoke. "You can only fill the pail with a set volume of water. Once the pail reaches full capacity the extra water spills over into the next pail. Likewise, once one tax bracket is full, the extra money spills over into the next tax bracket.

"Now, let's look at how your income gets distributed." He began scribbling numbers on the board. "Let's say your pension provides you $30,000 each year and Social Security provides another $25,000, along with $10,000 in interest and dividends from your investments. That adds up to $65,000 a year. This puts your last dollar in the 15% tax bracket."

"Okay," Katie said, "I'm following you so far."

"Just for argument's sake," the Guide said, "let's assume you withdraw $20,000 as an RMD from your IRA, making your annual income $85,000. That moves a portion of your income into the 25% tax bracket."[9] He wrote more notes on the board. "This

---

9 Based on 2013 Federal Income Tax Brackets.

gives you a chance to take advantage of one of the tax-savings strategies I'm talking about."

"What strategies can we use?" Ryan asked.

"Let's break down that hypothetical income of $85,000," the Guide said. He pointed to the 10% water pail. "Your income fills the lowest tax bracket initially. Your first $18,150 will be taxed at the 10% rate, which is when you reach your first threshold, the top of the water pail. Any income above that amount then spills over into the next 'tax pail.' Every dollar above that up to $73,800 will be taxed at the 15% tax rate, and the remainder up to the hypothetical $85,000 will be taxed at 25%. Does that make sense?"

They nodded thoughtfully.

"The tax bracket doesn't stop there, though," the Guide said. "The 25% tax bracket covers income between $73,800 and $148,850."[10]

"What does that mean for us," Katie asked.

"It means each year, provided your income is $85,000, you can withdraw an additional $63,850 without stepping into the next higher income tax bracket. Why leave your water pail only partially filled when the tax rate won't change? By using this strategy, you'll be able to withdraw money from your IRA at a faster pace without paying a higher percentage in taxes from year to year. You have the right to take advantage of the options within the tax code, and one of your options is withdrawing as much money as you can until that 'tax pail' is full.

---

10 IRS.gov (http://www.irs.gov/pub/irs-drop/rp-13-15.pdf)

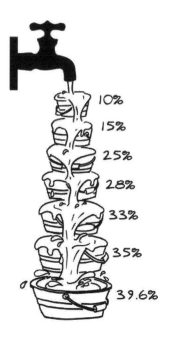

"In many situations, the more quickly you withdraw your money from your tax-deferred accounts, the sooner you can take advantage of tax-free accounts, and the fewer taxes you may end up paying in the long run. Tax laws and tax brackets can change. This year you may be in a 25% tax bracket, but next year, who knows? If you believe tax rates are rising, it may be wise to buy out your senior partner as soon as possible."

"I see," Katie said.

"This is where many people make a critical mistake," the Guide said. "There are two things that everyone should be aware of: what to do with the RMD if you're not going to use it and what to do with the additional money you are withdrawing. We find they often don't need the extra money they're required to withdraw from their IRA, so what is the best way to reinvest it? Unfortunately, many choose to reinvest it in savings accounts or other taxable investment accounts. You've already paid the tax on your IRA money, so why would you want to continue to pay taxes on your gains by investing in these types of accounts?"

"I'd never thought about that," Katie said.

The Guide smiled. "It's important to remember there are a number of tax-free strategies available to you, and you could reap great benefits by reviewing those strategies before making a decision with your money."

"That sounds great," Ryan said. "I'm certainly interested in buying out our senior partner early."

"Good. And these benefits are just scratching the surface. There are other implications to utilizing tax saving strategies now. This next point may be difficult to talk about, but I feel it's important to discuss," the Guide continued gently. "Eventually one of you will pass away and leave the other behind. It's unfortunate, but it happens to all of us. With the delicacy of the subject, some couples overlook this vital piece of their retirement plan."

"I guess you could say we've avoided that conversation," Ryan said, looking at his wife with a melancholy half-smile.

"That's alright," the Guide said. "Have you ever considered what would happen financially if one of you passed away?"

"I think whoever was left behind would be just fine," Katie said. "After all, our living cost would be reduced."

"That's sometimes true," the Guide replied, "but have you considered that your retirement income will drop as well?"

"What do you mean?"

"Many widows or widowers find it hard to adjust because their spouse was the one that took care of the budget, taxes and investments, etc... Sometimes they feel that they don't have enough to support themselves," the Guide said. "When one of you passes away, the remaining spouse will only receive the higher of the two social security checks that you previously received, which can reduce your retirement income significantly.

"Since you'll be filing as a single person instead of a married couple, the tax brackets are different and you may find yourself paying more in income taxes. You must also consider that, while being single lowers your living costs, it does not cut them in half. You may need additional income from your investments to compensate for reduced benefits and higher taxes."

"Wow," Ryan muttered, shocked. "I never thought so many factors would be involved when one of us passes away."

"With that in mind," the Guide continued, "wouldn't you like to take advantage of those tax saving strategies before those difficult single years arrive?"

"Now that you mention it, we definitely would," Katie replied, biting her lip.

"It would be important to buy out your senior partner earlier, and invest in tax-free accounts, giving both of you control while you are together.

"I didn't realize we had so many tax saving strategies available to us. We certainly need to take advantage of them if we want to stay ahead in our retirement years," Katie said.

"Believe me," the Guide added warmly, "you'll never regret being one step ahead."

CONVERTING TO A ROTH IRA WON'T BENEFIT YOU

"ONE OF THE MOST POPULAR tax-free accounts is the Roth IRA," the Guide said. "Now, before I begin telling you about the benefits of converting to a Roth IRA, let me reiterate that everybody's situation is different and that this particular strategy may not apply to everyone."

"What do you mean?" Ryan asked.

"Well, first of all, you have to understand that if you convert your IRA into a Roth IRA, you'll generally have to wait five years before touching the gains if you want them to be tax-free for growth and spending," the Guide replied. "That means that it probably wouldn't be the best investment for someone in their later years, in poor health, or needing income now. When converting to a Roth IRA, you want to have time on your side."

"Okay," Katie said. "So is it just about age?"

"Not *just*," the Guide said. "While age is an important factor to take into account, it's crucial to keep other things in mind such as your tax bracket, the current rate of inflation, your income needs and more."

"It sounds like there are quite a few factors to consider," Ryan said.

"That's right," the Guide replied. "Now, with the explanation out of the way, let's get down to the fun part. What can a conversion to a Roth IRA do for you?"

Katie eagerly leaned in.

"As you're taking the money from your IRA and converting those dollars into a Roth IRA, you'll notice some very distinct differences between the two accounts. In a Roth IRA, not only will you still have potential growth, but you'll also have full control of future tax obligations for you, your spouse and your heirs."

"What do you mean by control of future tax obligations? We'll still have to pay taxes on those accounts in the end, right?" Ryan asked.

"Actually no, because you already have," the Guide answered. "You see, when you withdraw the money from your IRA, you pay the tax on that money before converting it into the Roth account. The growth from your Roth IRA is now tax-free if you choose to use it for income, and whatever is left in the account will be passed on to your heirs tax-free as well."

"Sounds like a good idea," Katie said.

"Remember, when withdrawing money from your IRA, you want to make sure not to accidentally take too much and step into a higher tax bracket," the Guide said. "Let's not forget our water pails. Just as one too many drops of water can overflow into the next water pail, you need to be mindful of the exact amounts that each tax bracket contains. The difference between one tax bracket and another is just a matter of dollars.

"The tax bracket concept applies here as well. When you're converting, you want to make sure to look at all of your options. One is to convert as a lump sum and or another is to convert over a period of time. The key is to ensure you don't overpay on your income taxes."

"Let's say you both retire at 65," the Guide said. "The odds are that one of you is increasingly likely to live to at least 90 years old. In fact, according to the U.S. Census Bureau, 1.9 million Americans were 90 or older in 2010.[11] Katie, you are even more likely to reach 90 because women outnumber men in that age group 3 to 1."

"Wow," Katie said.

"My point is this," the Guide explained. "Just because you're retired, that doesn't mean you're 'done' improving and planning your life. You can't take a break from carefully considering your options with your money. Do you want your money to continue to grow over another 25 years or more in a tax-deferred IRA? Or would you prefer the option of having tax-free growth and income? Wouldn't that be a nice bonus during your retirement years?

"That certainly would be!" Katie exclaimed.

"Here's another point to consider. Every year, the IRS decreases your life expectancy and thus increases the RMD, or Required Minimum Distribution. A higher RMD withdrawal could potentially force you into taking more money out and even push you into a higher income tax bracket since you will be required to withdraw a higher percentage over the years. Rather than giving that control to the IRS, in most scenarios, you have the option to take back the control and have more freedom with a Roth IRA."

"Wow, I'd never thought about that before," Ryan said, nodding thoughtfully.

"The longevity trends also mean Ryan's chances of outliving Katie aren't good," the Guide said. "If Ryan passes away, Katie

---

11 United States Census Bureau. (http://www.census.gov/2010census/)

would be better taken care of if her income came from tax-free rather than taxable sources, and here's the reason why: If you passed away, Ryan, Katie's retirement income would likely be very similar to what you both receive. She would still be receiving the benefits of both of your retirement accounts. You'll also receive the higher of the two Social Security checks you currently receive. Unfortunately, when you file singly, the tax bracket cap amounts are cut in half. Essentially, her similar income would now put her in a higher tax bracket. She could potentially pay more in taxes because she'd be filing as a single person instead of as a married couple. I've seen it jump one or two tax brackets with that change alone. With money in taxable investments and with RMDs from your IRAs, the spouse left behind could wind up with a little less retirement income, and could suffer under a looming higher tax bracket.

"If you had a Roth IRA instead, Katie could more easily maintain her current lifestyle since the income is tax free."

Ryan reached over and held Katie's hand tightly, smiling gently at her. "I would definitely want her to keep all of her comforts."

"Interesting," Katie said. "That gives us quite an advantage, at least when it comes to taxes."

"That's right," the Guide replied. "Don't put this decision off any longer. Procrastination can potentially cost you thousands of dollars. The sooner you examine this option and determine whether it's right for you to convert a portion or all of your IRA to a Roth IRA, the more you may be able to enjoy your retirement to the fullest."

"I'm definitely concerned about that," Ryan said.

"That's because, along with your whole generation, you were raised to save your money," the Guide replied. "What many people don't realize is that retirement is exactly what their savings and investments are for. Remember, you can't take it with you.

Retirement is the time to really enjoy your life and fulfill all of your lifelong dreams you sacrificed before in order to save. You may want to travel, go golfing more often, go on a shopping spree every now and again, or even just visit your family more frequently. Whatever your heart desires, this is the time to do it."

Ryan and Katie looked at each other, both a little unsure.

"I'm not sure we know how to let go," Katie finally ventured.

"Many people feel the same way," the Guide said with a knowing smile. "They're hesitant to take that next step and really retire."

"What do you mean?" Ryan asked.

"I mean they think about money the same way they always have— as a vehicle to prepare for the future," the Guide said. "In retirement, though, money takes on a new role. You are now living your future. Money now helps you experience life."

"Experience life; I'd like that." Ryan sighed.

"I remember a wonderful couple who felt exactly the way you are both feeling now," the Guide said. "They were afraid they wouldn't have enough money to last the rest of their lives."

Ryan nodded.

"When I sat down with them," the Guide said, "we looked over their finances and discussed their lifestyle. We found that they had more money than they'd believed. You see, if an IRA to Roth conversion is right for you, you'll find there are three phases of benefits. The first phase, the most important one, is the benefit to you. The second phase is the benefit to whichever spouse lives longer. The third phase is the benefit to your heirs or whomever you choose to leave your money to when you both pass away.

"Let's focus on the first phase: the benefit to you. Once the conversion is complete, you no longer have to pay tax on your investment's growth, and, therefore, you may be able to enjoy your income from the long-term growth of your money, the money that would have gone to the IRS in taxes. Moving and converting those accounts creates smaller RMDs, leaving potentially fewer taxes not just on your IRAs over your lifetime but on your other income as well.

"So what's the rest of the story?" Katie asked. "What happened to the couple?"

"They enjoyed quite a few years together in retirement," the Guide said. "But the husband got very sick and he passed away. Of course, the experience of losing her spouse wasn't easy, but the planning we did helped her a lot because she didn't have to worry about the complications that would have arisen if they had kept their money in a traditional IRA.

"Shortly after his passing, the woman, who had never handled the finances during her marriage, came to me again. She was afraid to withdraw a rather small sum considering her overall investments. She wanted to travel to see her family because her grandson was receiving his Eagle Scout Award, something very important to her family. However, she didn't think she could afford to make the trip."

"What did she do?" Katie asked.

"Well, it was all about preparation. Not just her current preparation, but the measures she and her husband had taken years before to safeguard her future. We reviewed her plan. I reminded her that she and her husband had structured their accounts and benefits in order to get the most out of them years ago. After visiting with her and explaining the benefits," the Guide said, "she remembered that they had decided to convert from an IRA to a Roth Conversion which, in her case, gave her more income advantages over her lifetime. By preparing and putting their plan into place, she and her husband made sure that the surviving spouse could enjoy more dreams and have more fulfillment in the final years without worrying much about the financial side of things."

"Wow, I can see how planning ahead can really benefit us in the future!" Katie exclaimed, nudging Ryan. "We ought to see if a Roth Conversion would be a good fit for us. Did she fulfill her dream?"

"Yes, indeed, she took my advice and went on the trip to see her grandson receive his award. When the young man got up and told the story of how hard he'd worked, he did something unexpected," the Guide's voice choked with emotion as he moved toward the tan curtains. He pulled them back to reveal a ceremony with a young man at a podium in front of a supportive crowd. He was speaking with tears in his eyes as he suddenly motioned to his grandmother in the front row. Taken by surprise, she made her way up to the stage. Her grandson embraced her at the podium as she proudly took his arm.

"He thanked her for her support and encouragement, showing his appreciation by giving her the special Eagle Mentor pin. I can't tell you how wonderful it was for me to hear her story when she returned."

"Wow," Katie said, wiping her eyes. "What I would give to have an experience like that."

"You see," the Guide said, "she didn't think she could spend even a small part of her life savings in order to see her family for this very special event. If she hadn't made some of the right tax and investment decisions along the way, she might not have been able to. She needed that reminder to see what her life really could hold for her and what freedoms she could afford. Of course, every situation is different, but because we were able to prepare by converting the IRA into a Roth, providing her a tax-free income source, she was able to make that journey, and many more, and live her retirement years to the fullest. Imagine if she and her husband hadn't properly prepared their accounts with some guidance. She may have decided not to go on her trip, or she may not have been able to. Without converting to the Roth IRA, she would have only received 70 cents on the dollar, limiting her chances to take these trips. She may not have been able to share that beautiful experience with her grandson. But, because they converted their accounts and planned ahead, she held onto every tax-free dollar. She was able to make the trip and share a tender moment that I think she and her grandson will remember for the rest of their lives."

"That certainly is amazing," Ryan said with a happy sigh. "I'd love to start thinking further into the future so we can live some of our dreams, too."

"All you need is the proper guidance," the Guide said. "Many people have a bucket list of dreams they'd like to see come true. By looking at positioning your money in a tax-free account like a Roth IRA, you may be surprised how many of your own dreams may become reality."

ONE ACCOUNT CAN
SERVE ALL PURPOSES

"I HAVE A QUESTION ABOUT BENEFICIARIES," Katie said, deep in thought. "Of course we would like to provide a legacy for our children with our savings and investments after we're gone, but we also have a few charities we support, and we'd like to give some of our money to them as well."

"That's very generous of you," the Guide replied. "I'd like to begin by pointing something out that you may not have considered before.

"For the purposes of leaving behind a legacy, one account alone may not work. Did you know there's an array of ways to leave your assets behind, based on the type of account you chose? "It's important to consider how your children and your charity will receive your investments and plan accordingly. Many people choose to pass their IRAs to their children and leave other types of investments to charity. Your charity will receive the investment you give them tax-free, but your children won't. If you plan to leave your IRA investment to your children, remember the laws that govern it do not change. They will be under the same obligations you were to continue withdrawing RMDs based upon their own ages, unless you pass it down in one lump sum for them, which might not be your best option either. It's not just about leaving a legacy; it's about leaving that legacy in the most tax-efficient way, utilizing the right investments to possibly give your beneficiaries the full benefit they deserve."

"Interesting," Ryan said. "I never knew that was the case."

"Also, do you recall that there are several types of investments similar to an IRA including 401(k)s, 403(b)s, etc.? Well, what you may not be aware of is that there are several different types of IRAs as well. The possibilities are quite extensive," the Guide said with an excited grin.

"How do we know which one to use?" Katie asked, feeling a bit overwhelmed.

"It really depends on what you're trying to accomplish," the Guide answered. "Two of the biggest differences between IRAs and other similar accounts is first, how much money you're allowed to invest each year, and second, how you're able to pass the money on. Choosing your options is a bit like playing a game of chess." The Guide strode to the tan curtains and pulled them back to reveal a bird's eye view of a large chess board with two players hunched over an intense match. "Chess is a game of strategy – several sets of strategy, really. You not only need to understand your own pieces, and those of your opponent, but you also need to look forward. You need to plan several moves ahead of your current position, and you need to be flexible enough to alter those moves as the state of the board changes. So it is with your retirement accounts. You need a strategy to set up your accounts for yourself and for your future beneficiaries. How your accounts are passed on after you die can make a difference in the investments you chose now."

"Hum, so we need to strategize now what we want for our children and possibly even our grandchildren?" Katie asked.

"Why limit it to just that? Let's take Benjamin Franklin as an example. Benjamin Franklin was so efficient and strategic in setting up the way his legacy was passed on that the cities of Boston and Philadelphia are still benefiting from what he left behind."

"Wow," Ryan said. "Talk about staying a few moves ahead."

"There's more to setting up your IRA than simply naming your beneficiaries," the Guide said. "When you die, you want to maximize the benefit to each of your beneficiaries in the most tax-efficient way possible.

"Also, you can't use the same IRA to pass your money on to various people in different ways. Consider our chess example. You can't use your rook's straight movement to travel diagonally. If you're offering payouts to multiple individuals, it is best to have separate accounts."

"Why? How does that work?" Katie queried.

"Let's use your favorite charity as an example," the Guide said. "When you leave money to a charity, they often receive it as a lump sum. On the other hand, imagine leaving a lump sum to your children? Considering their spending habits, you may want to leave your IRA to them in a different way. Perhaps you'd like them to receive payouts every year over time, allowing the account time to grow. You see, by working out a system for separate payouts, you may be able to maximize their inheritance potential, making the account more beneficial for them in the long run. In that case, if the money for the charity and the money for your children are currently in the same account, you may need a second IRA in order to pass down money to your children differently if you so choose."

"That makes sense," Katie said.

"The bottom line is to determine how you'd like to pass your money on," the Guide said. "Would you rather give your beneficiary a lump sum, payments that are spread out over five years, ten years, a lifetime, or even until the IRA funds run out? These are just some of the options that everyone should consider and be aware of."

"Wow, I'd never given it that much thought," Ryan said, "but I can see we'll need to sit down and plan our next move more carefully. How will we know just how to configure our accounts and which options may be best?"

"There's no simple answer to that question," the Guide said. "The truth is there are several factors to consider: who you want to receive it, how you want them to receive it, how old your beneficiaries are, what tax brackets they fall under, what percentage you want to go to your children, what percentage goes to charity, etc... The options are nearly limitless with just as many factors to consider. With so many options, it's not hard to see that one account simply can't do it all."

"Well, we have our work cut out for us," Ryan said, giving Katie a glance. "We've never thought about the numerous ways we'd like our legacy passed on. Based on our beneficiaries' needs, we need to look at making some changes. I just can't wait to get started."

The Guide smiled and replied, "You're about to begin the process that will do so much good for you and your heirs in the future."

THERE'S ONLY ONE WAY TO LEAVE YOUR IRA BEHIND

⌒

KATIE SAT PONDERING FOR A moment. "I suppose I still have a big question in the back of my mind. What happens to our IRAs when we die? How would my husband and children receive it?"

"That's a perfect topic to discuss," the Guide replied. "A lot of people believe that when you pass away, your IRA is passed as a single taxable asset to your spouse," the Guide said. "What you may not realize is that if you do the proper planning, you can pass your IRA from spouse to spouse with no tax."

"Really?" Ryan asked.

"Yes! There are actually two available options. The first is called a spousal assumption. With this option, the surviving spouse assumes the IRA in name only as a non-taxable event. The second option is called a **spousal rollover** in which the IRA rolls over into the surviving spouse's current IRA," the Guide answered enthusiastically. "Keep in mind, though, that the surviving spouse will still be required to take RMDs, or Required Minimum Distributions, based on their age."

Ryan thought for a moment. "I have a question about that. Let's say the spouse who passed away was over 70 ½ and was already taking out RMDs regularly, but the surviving spouse was only 68. Would the RMDs for that transferred IRA stop until the surviving spouse reached the required age?"

"Good question," the Guide replied. "It actually depends on the calendar year in which the older spouse passed away. Let's take a hypothetical couple. Let's say John is 72 when he passed away, leaving Sue behind, who is 68. If John passed away, let's say in January, Sue would be required to take out the RMD for that year, since John had been alive within the calendar year. If John had already taken out his RMD and passed away in December, she would not need to withdraw the RMD at the turn of the year. Following that year, Sue wouldn't have to take any further distributions until she reached age 70½."

"Thank you," Ryan said. "That clears things up quite a bit. That spousal rollover option sounds really beneficial. Is there a spousal-like rollover option for our children as well?"

"I'm afraid not," the Guide said, "but, conveniently, there are many different ways to leave your IRA behind to your heirs." "There are?" Ryan asked.

"Oh yes, and you can choose the option to leave your IRA behind that best works for your children as individuals. As parents, I'm sure you've noticed that none of your children are exactly alike," the Guide said.

"You can say that again," Katie said with a chuckle.

"Though they grew up in the same house, with the same rules and expectations, they developed a wide range of personality traits, varying degrees of responsibility, and even various spending habits."

"We've definitely seen that in our own family," Ryan responded.

"I'm sure you have. Most parents can tell from an early age whether or not their children are going to be responsible with their money based on the decisions they've made and the habits they've formed early on.

"When they become adults, parents can really start to see these habits take shape. You've likely seen that your children end up being savers or spenders. The savers will put away a portion of every paycheck they receive toward their education, a house, an emergency savings account for a rainy day, or even towards investments for retirement. The spenders, on the other hand, usually have too much month at the end of their money. They live from paycheck to paycheck. Every extra dollar they earn is spent on a new gadget, a night out, or the latest trend, and they're not usually as financially stable as the savers."

"Hmm," Katie said.

"Like I said, the traits start early and could persist through adulthood or change over time. As your children age and mature, they may see the value of saving, or they might not. You know your children best in the end, and you can determine what plan would suit them individually.

"Knowing whether your child is a saver or a spender can make a big difference in how you choose to leave them your money. For example, children who are savers may benefit from a lump sum inheritance because they would tend to use it responsibly. They may invest it toward their own retirement plan. The spender, on the other hand, may buy a new car, a boat, or other large purchases that could quickly sap away those designated funds. In my personal experience, about half the children given an inheritance spend most of it within the first 3-18 months."

"That's incredible," Katie said. "An entire life savings gone, just like that?"

"It's a hard fact to hear, isn't it? With the right retirement guide, though, you can create a plan so your children can't go through your retirement savings so quickly," the Guide replied.

"I know we can limit their access to our money now," Ryan said, "but other than cutting them out of our will entirely, how can we have that same control after we're gone?"

"That's an excellent question," the Guide replied, "and one answer is a Stretch IRA. The Stretch IRA is a win-win way to set up an investment. Not only do you have better control of the way your heirs can access the money you leave behind, but it may also save them money on taxes."

"Is that really possible?" Katie asked.

"Absolutely," the Guide replied. "Let me explain how it works. With proper planning, the IRA's value won't be paid to your heirs in one lump sum."

"How does it work, then?" Ryan asked.

"With a Stretch IRA, the funds are paid out in small increments, similar to the RMD, based upon your child's age, life expectancy, and the Required Minimum Distributions that they would be required to receive as a beneficiary. If set up correctly, the Stretch IRA has the potential to do just that: it can stretch your IRA money throughout most, if not all, of your child's life.

"You see, passing down your IRA in one lump sum is a lot like giving your children all of their Halloween candy at once. I'm not sure if there are many kids out there who would calmly nibble a few pieces of candy and replace the rest for later. More likely, if allowed, they'll feast on that candy until they're practically sick.

"As parents, we know that our children would certainly love to have the candy all at once, but is that really what's best for them?

A huge payout is like a looming candy temptation that could give even the most responsible adults a hankering for sweets. What they'll appreciate more in the long run is the chance an extended pay-out plan gives them to use the money wisely. Keep in mind, however, that your children do still have the option available to take the entire amount at once should they so choose."

Katie chuckled a bit. "I never would have thought about it that way. How are the payments divided up? Are they set amounts like the RMDs?" Katie asked.

"Let's take a look at an example." The Guide slid back the wooden panel on the wall to reveal the white board again. "Let's imagine that when you pass away, your child is 50 years old. According to the life expectancy chart used in IRS Publication 590 that child's life expectancy would be 34.2 years. Assuming the value of your IRA is $250,000, the first payment would be calculated based on that life expectancy. It would look like this:" The Guide wrote the following on the board:

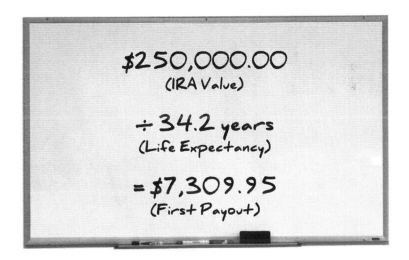

$250,000.00
(IRA Value)

÷ 34.2 years
(Life Expectancy)

= $7,309.95
(First Payout)

"I'm beginning to see now. Does that calculation apply to every payment? Wouldn't every payment be the same in that case?"

"Not exactly," the Guide replied. "You see, the Life Expectancy Table that the IRS uses changes the life expectancy of an individual every year. Naturally, as you get older, the years you are likely to live decreases. For instance, we mentioned that your child is hypothetically 50 years old when you pass away, so his or her life expectancy is 34.2 years."

"That's right," Katie said, nodding.

"Upon turning 51, the life expectancy decreases to 33.3, so about a year less. Based on that information and a hypothetical 3% rate of return on your IRA, the new balance would be $249,887." The Guide turned back to the white board to pen the second formula. "Thus, the second payment would look like this." He scribbled on the board again:

$$\$249,887$$
(New IRA Value, based on 3% rate of return)

$$\div 33.3 \text{ years}$$
(New Life Expectancy)

$$= \$7,504.12 \text{ (Second Payout)}$$
*This is an increase of $194.17 from the previous year

"So, the payments could continue to increase over time?" Ryan asked.

"It's certainly a possibility, but there are more factors at play. Remember, these numbers are based on the IRS Life Expectancy Table," the Guide said, "but they're also tied to the gains and losses of your IRA in the market. Based on the consistent 3% rate of return we discussed, the amount paid out would increase for a few years."

"Okay, that makes sense," Katie said. "I do have a question, though. What happens if our children do not reach the life expectancy projected in the table? If they pass away before they receive the full value of the IRA, what happens to the money they would have received?"

"Good question," the Guide replied. "If there is any money left over, the money would go to their designated beneficiaries."

"Wow," Katie said. "I can see there's a lot more to leaving our money behind than I realized. I know that life expectancy changes over the years. Does that ever make a difference in that chart?" "That's a good question. The table being used today hasn't changed for many years and is unlikely to change in the future, but it is possible. Your retirement guide can keep you up-to-date with any changes that affect you and your investments."

"This type of IRA would give us so much peace of mind!" Ryan said emphatically. "Could our grandchildren benefit from a Stretch IRA as well?" Ryan said.

"Of course they could," the Guide replied. "Let me share an example with you. Imagine, when you both pass away, your IRA is valued at $250,000. Let's use a single child and single grandchild as an example." The Guide excitedly moved over to the white board and began scribbling the notes. "If you decide to leave 80% to your child and 20% to your grandchild in one lump sum, your child would receive a total of $200,000 minus taxes and your grandchild would receive the remaining $50,000 minus taxes.

"Now, let's take that same amount and distribute it in annual payments with a potential to last over their lifetime through a Stretch IRA. Your child's 80% over their lifetime becomes $353,858 minus taxes, and your grandchild's 20% becomes $134,562 minus taxes."

"That's incredible," Katie said.

"That's more than double the original value of the IRA," Ryan exclaimed.

"Of course these numbers are just an example and every situation will be a little bit different. Just as with everything we've discussed so far, your IRA must be set up properly in order to efficiently benefit your grandchildren the same way it does your children."

"How do we do that?" Katie asked.

"Well, keep in mind that a Stretch IRA is designed to be passed down to your child, who we'll say is 50 years old for the sake of the example," the Guide said. "Let's imagine you'd also like to pass the money down to your grandchild as well within the same Stretch IRA account. Here's what would happen. Let's assume your grandchild is 26 years old. Because of the way the Stretch IRA is set up, your grandchild will receive the same percentage of distributions for their share as your 50-year-old child, meaning the life expectancy will be the same for both the child and grandchild: 32.2 years. Based on that table, your grandchild could run out of distributions at the same time your child does."

"What would you suggest we do instead?" Ryan asked.

"Well," the Guide said, "according to the life expectancy table, the life expectancy for a 26-year old is 57.2 years. So in this particular scenario, using the same IRA would not be as beneficial for your grandchild as for your child. I think the best way to handle it is to do what we discussed previously— create a separate account to leave behind to your grandchild.

"That's what is so wonderful about the ways you can allocate your accounts. You have a wide variety of options, including specifically designed trusts within these IRA options."

"That's wonderful," Katie said.

"Again, remember, there are several options and situations to keep in mind," the Guide said. "It's important you work with a retirement guide to know which option best fits you and your heirs."

"Wow. You're right!" Katie exclaimed. "I can't believe there are so many ways to leave our IRAs behind and give our family so many advantages. We could have so much more confidence when we leave our money to our heirs!"

"I'm glad you can see just how valuable all of this knowledge can be for you and your heirs," the Guide replied warmly.

ONCE YOUR BENEFICIARIES ARE SET UP, YOU'RE DONE

⌒

"Even though this is one of the last things we're discussing today," the Guide said, "designating your beneficiaries is one of the most crucial things to do correctly with regards to your IRA."

"Really?" Ryan asked with a spark of curiosity, glancing at Katie. "We thought that was the easy part."

"Many people assume the same thing, and that's the reason slight errors can occur when it comes to setting up your beneficiary designations," the Guide answered. "In fact, in my experience, about 70% of the people with whom I've visited initially had their beneficiaries set up incorrectly."

"That many?" Katie asked, astonished. "I always thought the process of designating beneficiaries was straightforward. How do people make misinformed decisions?"

"Sometimes the errors can be small and the arrangement of beneficiaries just needs a few adjustments or tweaks," the Guide said. "In other cases, the seemingly minor flaws could potentially cost your beneficiaries hundreds or even thousands of dollars."

"Wow," Ryan said. "What kind of flaws are we talking about?"

"The first and biggest mistake you can make is not setting up beneficiaries at all, assuming that your estate will be passed on exactly as you wish with no problems."

"I can't see too many people making that mistake," Katie said, laughing.

"You'd be surprised," the Guide answered. "Before I met some of my clients, they invested in IRAs when they were young and simply continued to put off setting up their beneficiaries. After years of procrastination, they may have forgotten about it altogether."

Ryan nodded.

"Another big mistake you can make when it comes to your IRA is not reviewing your beneficiaries regularly," the Guide said. "Allow me to share a story I read in the New York Post some time ago about a woman who made this mistake. The story is about her retirement account, but the same scenario could happen with an IRA.

"When this woman set up her retirement account, she named her mother, uncle and sister as her beneficiaries. Four years later, she met her husband on a blind date. They were married for twenty years before she passed away. Here's the catch. She had never updated her beneficiary form and, because of that oversight, her husband was left destitute while his sister-in-law, the only living beneficiary on the woman's form, received her retirement account benefits which were nearly $1 million."

The Guide pulled back the tan curtains to reveal a somber courtroom. An older gentleman sat before the judge, a haggard look on his face. An attorney was hard at work gesturing and explaining, seemingly to no avail under the steady gaze of the stone-faced judge.

"The man even tried to contest it with the Manhattan Supreme Court, but they ruled in favor of the sister-in-law, stating the wife's intention to make her husband the beneficiary couldn't be assumed and the paperwork had to be honored as filed.[12]"

The harsh sound of the gavel smacking the pulpit reverberated throughout the room. Ryan and Katie gave a startled jump.

"Wow, that must have been difficult," Katie said.

"You see," the Guide said, continuing, "setting up your beneficiaries incorrectly can cause more than financial problems. Imagine how this happily-married man felt when he found out that his wife left her pension to his sister-in-law. I imagine there's a lot of hurt and anger behind that story, and the incident more than likely tore a rift in the family."

"I can only imagine," Ryan said, considering if he were in the man's position.

"Sadly enough, the woman set up those beneficiaries correctly in the first place. But, she neglected to regularly review them, and that is how this costly mistake crept in. Often, after you've filled out your beneficiary forms, the problem isn't that you've done something wrong. The problem is that life happens, and certain events can affect how and to whom you'd like your legacy to be passed down."

"What major events should we watch out for?" Katie asked.

"It's best to review those beneficiaries any time something occurs to change your family dynamic. For example, imagine if you were previously divorced and forgot to update the form," the Guide said. "You could accidentally leave a nice living to your ex-spouse and leave only hurt and anger for your current spouse. What if you name your grandchildren on the beneficiary form but before you pass away, another grandchild is born, and you neglect

---

12 New York Post (http://nypost.com/2005/01/31/pension-pickle-broke-widower-loses-1m-to-in-law/)

to update the form? How will that youngest grandchild feel if he or she is the only one who didn't receive part of your legacy?"

"That's true," Ryan said. "We should probably double check our beneficiary forms to make sure all of our grandchildren are listed."

"That would be a good idea. If waiting for a family dynamic change seems like a difficult schedule to follow, it's wise to review all of your beneficiaries on a regular basis since these mistakes are so common," the Guide said.

"One of the more common mistakes I've seen in my personal experience is related to your primary beneficiary. Sometimes spouses forget to name the other as the primary beneficiary. I've seen this happen in two ways. I've seen the children listed as primary beneficiaries and the spouse listed as a secondary, or contingent beneficiary. However, I've also seen a complete oversight of the spouse altogether. The husband or wife designates the children as the beneficiaries. They assume that the accounts automatically default to the spouse first or that the beneficiary form only comes into play after both spouses have passed away.

"An even more common error I run into is neglecting to name a secondary beneficiary altogether. That's one of biggest mistakes you can make. A couple may designate a spouse or their children as the primary beneficiaries but leave the secondary beneficiary blank. In the event that the primary beneficiary is not around to receive the inheritance, you can imagine the fiasco involved when a secondary beneficiary hasn't been named."

"I guess it's more important than I thought to stay current with our beneficiary designations," Katie said.

"Keep in mind," the Guide said, "these are only a few of the more common examples of things that could go wrong. There are several more you may need to be aware of depending on your family dynamic. I recommend you review your beneficiaries regularly with a retirement guide to make sure your heirs and assets are protected from easily-made mistakes."

Katie pursed her lips thoughtfully. "I was wondering, though, what's the best way to pass down our IRAs fairly and equally among all our children and grandchildren?"

"Let's see. One of the ways I'd recommend to make sure your money is passed on to your heirs fairly is to follow the bloodline," the Guide answered. "For example, using the correct methods, you can set up your beneficiary designations so that if one of your children should pass away before you, their share of your legacy would be passed on to their children rather than being divided among the other siblings."

"Interesting," Ryan said.

"After all is said and done, keep in mind the most important part. You should have one primary goal when passing on your IRA:" the Guide emphasized. "having it done *your* way! You have the chance and privilege to leave *your* money to the family or charities *you* want, precisely the way *you* want to, all through the most tax-efficient method possible."

"Thank you. You've given us a chance to understand what our own simple beneficiary errors might be. I can see why we need to review those accounts on a regular basis with the right guide," Katie added with a sigh of relief.

"That's right," the Guide replied. "We're just scratching the surface, here. A careful analysis of your accounts on a frequent basis can really go a long way in making you feel safe and secure about your financial planning," the Guide said, smiling.

ANY FINANCIAL
ADVISOR WILL DO

$\backsim$

"I'M SURE YOU'VE NOTICED A little repetition throughout the course of the afternoon," the Guide said, chuckling. "With nearly every piece of advice I've given, I've mentioned that you need to work with the right retirement guide. Now, I'd like to discuss that particularly. Believe me, one of the most important things you can do is pick the right person to work with to plan your financial future," the Guide said. "There is no jack-of-all-trades when it comes to financial professionals. Just as no doctor can take care of every medical condition, no financial professional has the same expertise as another."

"What do you mean?" Katie asked.

"Well, there are broker dealers who work primarily with stocks, bonds and mutual funds, and a few other accounts," the Guide said. "There are also insurance agents who focus more on life, annuities or medical insurance. It is important to look for advisors who carry licenses to cover both categories. Working with a guide who only carries one of these licenses can put you at a disadvantage. They won't legally be able to discuss the other category of accounts, so you could potentially miss out on the best tools to construct your financial plan."

Ryan nodded, thoughtfully.

"Of course there are also retirement guides, more commonly known as financial advisors. Within this category, there are two main types of advisors. First, there are those who work for companies who are captive advisors. The companies require them to offer proprietary products with some or all of their investments. Basically, captive financial advisors primarily seek to sell their products first whenever possible. If they simply can't find the right fit with their investment products, some may defer to other financial companies, but they usually exhaust all of their own financial avenues first. Second, there are independent advisors who aren't tied down to a specific company and generally have more options available to them."

"So independent advisors do things differently than those who work for companies, but what's so important about that difference? Why does that matter when I choose an advisor?" Katie asked.

"I'm glad you asked," the Guide replied. "Independent advisors help you shape the retirement plan you desire, but instead of trying to fit you into a company's financial model, they search for the company that best fits you. They help you build that financial house we discussed earlier."

"I remember," Ryan said, "but I'm not sure I fully understand the concept of the financial house."

"The financial house is a way to invest your money while protecting your assets." The Guide jumped up and strolled to the window to reveal a final scene. They gazed at an open construction site, prepared and ready for building. "Just like building a regular house, you lay the cornerstone first." Four thick blocks materialized at each of the four corners of the house's foundation.

"When you mentioned the cornerstones before," Katie said, "you said they were for protecting your assets. What exactly are the cornerstones?"

"Well, the first cornerstone represents savings. I recommend you keep at least 3-12 months of wages set aside for emergencies. The next cornerstone represents protection for your assets, meaning insurance on your homes, auto, and other assets. The third cornerstone represents protecting yourself, which means setting up healthcare insurance, Medicare, Long-Term-Care, home healthcare, etc. The last cornerstone represents protecting your spouse and heirs. This can include life insurance for debt and income replacement, and final expenses for funeral costs."

"Interesting," Ryan said thoughtfully.

"After your cornerstones are in place, you focus on the foundation." Thick cement materialized between the cornerstones, creating a large square awaiting the rest of the structure. "This represents safe, secure investments. These are the investments you have outside the market. The market ebb and flow will have no effect on these investments. Though they may not yield huge interest gains at times, they remain strong even when the market is weak. Once you feel your foundation is sturdy, you move on to the walls of the home, or what I refer to as low-risk, low-volatility investments." Four large brick-lain walls emerged from the base of the structure. "For your low-risk accounts, your goals are to move your investments to cash in a downward market, to avoid going backwards on your investments over time, and to help your investments keep pace with inflation. After you feel comfortable with these investments, then you can focus on the roof to potentially make more money with moderate to high-risk investments." The roof appeared, completing the financial house.

"Here's a question for you," the Guide asked thoughtfully. "Let's say you wanted to build a new home. Would you draw up the blueprints, purchase materials, and begin construction without having any knowledge of construction work?"

"Certainly not!" Katie exclaimed. "That would be ridiculous."

"I agree," replied the Guide. "Attempting it would result in a poorly-made structure at best, not to mention all of the unnecessary worry that would go along with it. Instead, you hire a contractor and a construction team to ensure the house will be sound, sturdy, and well-made. That's the best option right?"

"Sounds like it to me," Ryan chimed in.

"Well, the same principles apply to your financial house. Building a financial plan alone is like constructing a house without a contractor. You may be able to work out the basics, but when it comes to creating a secure, steady, and well-crafted financial plan, it's best to leave the job to the right financial guide. That's why it's so important to build your financial plan correctly, so that you can both diversify your accounts and keep them strong.

"Okay, that makes a lot of sense," Ryan said. "So how do we know what guide will be best to work with while we build our financial house?"

"Well, on the specific topic of IRAs, you want a guide who stays up-to-date on IRA news and law changes. Does he or she keep up with the *IRS Publication 590*? With all of the frequent changes that occur, you'll need a keen eye and a listening ear on your side."

"Hmm," Katie said, thinking. "It makes sense to work with someone who knows the most current laws."

"Precisely," the Guide agreed. "Next, I would learn what licenses your guide has. Financial professionals are bound by many laws and, without the proper licensing, they cannot offer or even discuss certain products or services which may be valuable to your overall retirement plan. You don't want to miss out on anything.

"You also want to make sure you understand your guide's investment philosophy. One example of this is the financial house I just mentioned. Some advisors may be too conservative for you; others may be too risk-oriented. It's important to find a guide who is willing to work within your personal risk-tolerance level."

"Another important factor is whether or not your guide is local. You see, it's easier to get in touch with your retirement guide if he or she has a local office and telephone number. It's important to know how invested your guide is in your community. Can you imagine working with a financial professional who worked too far away to visit with in person?"

"Well," Ryan said, "we did that for a while because we moved away and felt our guide was still a great asset."

"I'm glad he was helping you so much," the Guide replied, "but what about your bank? Did you keep your money in the same bank when you moved?"

"No," Katie said, shaking her head. "Ours wasn't a national bank, so they didn't have a branch here locally."

"Alright. That tells me that you knew it was important to keep your money with a local establishment, so that you could work with your bankers in person. It's important to treat your IRA money, or any other type of investment, that same way," the Guide said. "Knowing you can get together face to face with the person managing your finances can offer peace of mind that you can lose over a long distance."

"Wow," Ryan replied, running his hand through his hair. "I suppose you're right."

The Guide responded reassuringly, "You see, even though we've covered a lot of information today, we've only gotten through the basics of IRAs and other similar investments. There's still so much information out there that can help you. Working with the right guide, who has the proper financial education and experience, can make a huge difference in the success of your retirement plan."

"Wow, I'm so glad we know just how important it is to work with the right financial guide for us. We look forward to our next visit," Ryan said with feeling.

The Guide grasped Ryan's shoulder, "Believe me, I too look forward to our next visit, and I'm here to guide you."

THE PACKET

"It's been more than a pleasure to talk with both of you," the Guide said. "Before you go, I'd like to give you something."

He stood and walked over to a bookshelf, pulled a small folder from one of the shelves and put it on the table in front of Ryan and Katie.

"What's this?" Ryan asked.

"It's a small packet summarizing everything we've just talked about," the Guide said. "We've discussed how we can shatter 13 misconceptions about IRAs, so in this packet, I've rewritten them. These are now the 13 truths about IRAs that you can carry with you as a reminder of everything we discussed. That way you won't have to remember everything." The Guide nudged them playfully and gave them a wink.

"Good," Katie said, chuckling, "sometimes we forget."

They all laughed.

Ryan and Katie opened the folder and began to read:

13 Truths About IRAs

Truth #1:
Your IRA may be yours, but the government has most the control.

Truth #2:
You WILL pay tax on your IRA. How you choose to take back control will determine how much you pay.

Truth #3:
There are a few strategies to withdraw money from your IRA before age 59½ without being subject to a penalty.

Truth #4:
Your IRA has more investment options available than your 401(k).

Truth #5:
You should treat your IRA differently in retirement than you did during your career.

Truth #6:
Missing an RMD could cost you hundreds or
even thousands of dollars, so don't forget.
Make sure your RMD is sent to you annually.

Truth #7:
Too many accounts can be overwhelming,
so consolidate as much as possible.

Truth #8:
There are tax savings strategies that apply to your IRA and,
with proper planning, they will work for you.

Truth #9:
Converting your IRA into a Roth IRA has several benefits for
you, your spouse, and your heirs.

Truth #10:
If you plan to leave a legacy to more than one
beneficiary, it may be necessary to have more than one account.

Truth #11:
There are several options when it comes
to leaving your money behind.

Truth #12:
Review your beneficiaries on a regular basis to
keep them correct and up-to-date.

Truth #13:
Make sure you work with the right retirement guide.

CONCLUSION

A FTER A WARM FAREWELL, RYAN and Katie left the conference room feeling more confident than they had that morning. They knew they had finally been educated so they could really capitalize on their IRA accounts and make the most of their retirement. Katie squeezed Ryan's hand as they got into their car.

"Well, where to now?" she asked a bit playfully.

Looking ahead, Ryan and Katie saw the road stretch before them and felt like they hadn't finished a journey, but that they were actually just beginning.

Bonus Misconception A
2014 Tax Court Ruling

IN THE LATE STAGES OF writing this book, there was a Tax Court ruling to clarify a previously misunderstood portion of the once-per-year IRA rollover rule. Rather than delay the release of this book, I have decided to share this information with you in a more straightforward manner here at the end of the book.

Many people (including IRA experts and financial advisors) believed the once-per-year rollover rule applied to each individual's IRA, meaning you could withdraw money from your IRA and roll it over into another tax-free as long as it was done within a 60-day period. This could be done once per IRA.

The IRS and Tax Court have informed us (as of January 28, 2014) that this belief is incorrect. The once-per-year rollover rule applies to ALL of an individual's IRAs, meaning whether you have 1 IRA or 10 IRAs, you may still only use a tax-free 60-day rollover period once per year.

Please note that the IRS has defined the "year" as from the original date when the distribution was taken and not as a calendar year. This means if you perform one rollover in December, you cannot do another in January. You will have to wait until December to perform your next IRA rollover.

Also, bear in mind this ruling does not change the number of IRA-to-IRA direct transfers you may do in a year. It only affects the 60-day transfers where you withdraw the money and deposit it yourself.

About Eric L. Scott

⟝⟞

Eric L. Scott is the President and founder of Eric Scott Financial. He has served in the financial industry since 1983 and enjoys sharing the knowledge he's gained through his many years of experience.

Eric hosts a weekly radio program on KDXU 890 AM in Saint George, Utah every Tuesday morning at 8:30am called "Financial Crossroads". He also teaches financial courses to the community through Dixie State University's Community Education department.

In 2011, Eric was invited to contribute as a financial expert in nationally recognized investment advisor and radio talk show host "Coach Pete" J. D'Arruda's financial advice book, *Have You Been Talking to Financial Aliens?*

In August 2012, Eric released his own financial advice book entitled *The Five Crossroads: Unlocking the Secrets to Your Retirement Journey* which explains his retirement planning philosophy using a unique storytelling experience.

At home, Eric loves spending time with his family and is active in his church, his community, and the Boy Scouts of America. He and his wife have been married since 1979 and currently reside in Saint George, Utah. He enjoys spending time with his children and grandchildren. In his leisure time, Eric enjoys swimming, exploring the red rocks on his ATVs and enjoying the outdoors.

Eric Scott Financial
43 S. 100 E. Ste. #201
Saint George, UT 84770
Phone: (435)773-9444
Email: info@ericscottfinancial.com
www.ericscottfinancial.com

Made in the USA
San Bernardino, CA
26 February 2015